GOD'S FANTASTIC CREATION

GOD'S FANTASTIC CREATION

MURIEL LARSON

moody press
chicago

© 1975 by
THE MOODY BIBLE INSTITUTE
OF CHICAGO

All rights reserved.

Library of Congress Catalog Card Number: 75-12511

ISBN: 0-8024-3033-3

Printed in the United States of America

CONTENTS

Chapter	Page
1. God's Creation Testifies of God	7
2. The Universe	19
3. Little Things	31
4. The Mighty Sea	42
5. The Plant World	54
6. Insects and Arachnids	76
7. Sea Creatures	90
8. Reptiles and Amphibians	104
9. The Birds	120
10. Beasts of the Field	139
11. The Miracle of Mankind	156
12. The New Creation	180
Bibliography	187

Acknowledgment

I wish to express my appreciation to George Mulfinger, science professor at Bob Jones University, for his verification of the authenticity of the scientific facts presented in this book.

1

GOD'S CREATION TESTIFIES OF GOD

For ever since the creation of the world His invisible nature and attributes, that is, His eternal power and divinity have been made clearly discernible in and through the things that have been made—His handiworks (Ro 1:20, Amp.).

CREATION RICH IN EVIDENCE

ALL OF GOD'S CREATION is rich in the evidence of His existence and His handiwork. One needs only to really look at various plants and creatures to know that behind such intricate design and practicality there must be a supreme intelligence.

Beginning with the most magnificent creation of God, the universe, most of us know that there is a definite pattern in it all. If it were not so, we would not know from one night to the next where the stars and planets would be. If it were not so, planets and stars would be crashing into each other constantly, and our own planet would have been short-lived. Who made the laws by which the movements of stars, planets, and our solar system are ruled?

Astronomers know that all the stars, solar systems, galaxies, and comets have a definite pattern of movement. What supermathematician planned all this? The Bible asks:

> Who hath measured the waters in the hollow of his hand, and meted out heaven with the span, and comprehended the dust of the earth in a measure, and weighed the mountains in scales, and the hills in a balance? (Is 40:12).

God Himself asks:

> Canst thou bind the sweet influences of Pleiades, or loose the bands of Orion? Canst thou bring forth Mazzaroth [the twelve signs] in his season? Or canst thou guide Arcturus with his sons? Knowest thou the ordinances of heaven? Canst thou set the dominion thereof in the earth? (Job 38:31-33).

Our solar system alone is a marvel of design. According to scientists, the nine planets that swing around our sun are at precisely the right distance from each other. Further, the planet on which we humans live is at exactly the right distance from the sun, so that it neither gets too hot nor too cold for us to live, as it does on the other planets. The Bible says that God set the sun and the moon in the firmament of heaven (Gen 1:17). The sun is constantly in movement, as is our planet. Yet we stay precisely the same comfortable distance from this source of life and light.

Even as we see the evidence of the existence of an intelligent, interested, and mighty God in the vastness of creation, so we see it in the little things all around us.

"Hast thou entered into the treasures of the snow?" God asked Job over 3,000 years ago. It has only been comparatively recently that man has been able to do just that, with the aid of a microscope. Scientists say that no two snowflakes are alike. Every one of the millions of snowflakes that have fallen, and will fall, are of a six-sided geometric design, yet no two are alike!

Science also has discovered within the last hundred years the multitudes of microbes, bacteria, and viruses that exist in our world, each tiny living thing the cause of some process that occurs. They have just recently discovered that the microscopic atom can be split, and tremendous power comes from such a splitting. It also has been verified that there is infinitely more space in solid-appearing objects than there is matter!

The earth and the multitude of blessings for man that it contains are testimonies to the creation of God. The climate of earth is ideal for the existence of man; in fact, scientists say that it appears to be the only planet in our solar system on which man and animals are able to live. The atmosphere and gravity of our planet are just right for man. Plenty of water and sunlight are provided for him. God placed on earth all kinds of trees, plants, and flowers as well as animals and fish; these provide man with a wonderful variety of food, clothing, shelter, and beauty.

There are minerals and metals of every kind for man's happiness and welfare: gold, silver, precious gems, iron, copper, brass, marble, aluminum, silica, coal, gas, oil, radium, and cobalt. God has even made the principle of electricity available to man, with all its related blessings and comforts. The earth with its storehouse of treasures did not "just happen," any more than has one of our fabulous World's Fairs. These fairs are the result of intelligent minds and much planning. So, too, the earth is the creation of the greatest intelligence of all: God.

A good part of the earth is covered by the sea, a sea filled with a multitude of miracles and treasures. It is a veritable storehouse of life, minerals, and food for mankind. "They that go down to the sea in ships, that do business in great waters; these see the works of the LORD, and his wonders in the deep" (Ps 107:23-24).

Man has never yet solved all the grand mysteries of the great seas that God made. The currents, the tides, the evaporation, the life therein: all are in the sea by God's command and creation, for the good of earth and man.

Consider also the unique and amazing compatability of every beast, reptile, fish, and bird with its environment. The Bible says:

> But ask now the beasts, and they shall teach thee; and the fowls of the air, and they shall tell thee: or speak to the earth, and it shall teach thee: and the fishes of the sea shall declare unto thee. Who knoweth not in all these that the hand of the LORD hath wrought this? In whose hand is the soul of every living thing, and the breath of all mankind (Job 12:7-10).

There are thousands of species in each of these categories. There are animals which are well-fitted to thrive in the far north and those just as well-fitted to live in their environment near the equator. Fish and birds are similarly equipped. In addition, God has given every one of His creatures in these categories instincts that are absolutely necessary to their survival. Their species would never have continued to exist if they had not been so equipped from the very beginning.

Strange as it may seem, most of the sometimes repulsive and sometimes gorgeous insect species have been proved to be necessities in God's balance of nature on earth. Many of them are absolutely indispensable for the fertilization of plants, trees, and flowers. Most provide a very necessary source of food for birds, and a number have their own little specialized tasks as well. Have you ever studied the perfect design on the backs of some insects or on the wings of butterflies and moths? These perfect designs had a master Designer.

Have you ever examined the intricate design in flowers and leaves? The petals of flowers come in many lovely shapes: smooth, broken, pointed, blunt, forked, cusped, or ragged. The formal florets of the dahlia, the feather pink, the star-shaped gilia, the bell-shaped lily, the trumpet-shaped petunia, and the three-point trillium have served as inspiration for mankind's talented designers. Who equipped so many of these creations of beauty with their exquisite and individual fragrances? Was it not our God of love? Yes, God was the Originator of wonderful designs and delectable perfumes!

Man himself is a testimony to God. A unique creature in all the earth, man has the brainpower to create and invent a tremendous variety of necessities and conveniences for himself. Man's body is a marvel of design, composed of at least 5,000 named anatomical parts. The Bible says: "Know ye that the LORD he is God: it is he that hath made us, and not we ourselves" (Ps 100:3).

Man still has not figured himself out, but he learns more all the time. He has learned, for instance, that many parts of himself that he used to consider useless do serve some very necessary function.

The Bible says that man was made in the image of God (Gen 1:27). We have, like God, a personality consisting of self-consciousness, intelligence, and free will. Man was also created a moral being with a conscience. Some have so quelled their consciences that they are no longer bothered by them. But after we have received Christ as our Saviour, we are more acutely aware of right and wrong than ever before.

The awesome beauty of God's earth and heavens has caused many a man to think about the existence of God. The riotous color of a garden of flowers; the magnificence and spectacular blend of hues of mountains and canyons; the gorgeous magenta, lavender, and gold of a sunset; the miraculous appearance of a rainbow in the sky; the flash of red or blue on wing; the coloratura sparkling forth from a tiny mocking bird; the luxuriousness of a mink's fur; the crashing of a powerful surf on a beach; the ripples of the water in sunlight; the quiet touching beauty of a full moon; the sky full of stars; a cooing baby; a mother's tender smile; a father's gentle solicitude; a thousand things of beauty for eye, ear, and touch all say, "There is a God, a God who cares!" "The heavens declare the glory of God; and the firmament sheweth his handywork" (Ps 19:1).

Rich in Comparisons

The Bible is rich in comparisons between the things of God's creation and things in the spiritual realm.

The Lord Jesus Christ, God's Son, is called the Lily of the Valley, the Rose of Sharon, the Lamb that taketh away the sin of the world, the Lion of the tribe of Judah, the light, the life, the rock, and the bread of life. He came into the world as a tiny helpless baby in order to identify Himself with mankind; then He grew to boyhood and manhood without ever sinning, according to the Bible.

The Bible says, "The Word became flesh [Jesus Christ] and dwelt among us" (Jn 1:14). This was the only way God could bridge the gap that had been created between Himself and man by man's disobedience and sin. Through the perfect obedience of one man, who was God Himself, the gap was bridged, and righteousness is imputed to all those who believe in Him and accept His sacrifice for their sins. Thus, basic to the plan of salvation was the incarnation of God in human flesh. He Himself, as He walked on this earth, used many illustrations from among the things of His own creation.

Jesus pointed to the lilies of the field, noting how beautifully they were clothed; He reminded His disciples that if God clothed the short-lived lilies so well, surely He would provide their clothing, without their having to worry about it. He pointed to the sparrows and said that not one of them fell to the ground without God's knowledge. He told His disciples that if one little sparrow meant so much to God, surely the welfare of His disciples meant infinitely more.

Jesus came to a fig tree, looking for fruit. There was nothing but leaves on the tree. It was condemned by Christ and died, a reminder through the ages that those who profess to be the Lord's people should be bearing fruit. As they passed through a field of wheat, Jesus said to His disciples, "Except a corn of wheat fall into the ground and die, it abideth alone: but if it die, it bringeth forth much fruit." Then he added the spiritual application: "He that loveth his life shall lose it; and he that hateth his life in this world shall keep it unto life eternal" (Jn 12:24-25).

When Jesus met the woman at the well, her mind was on drinking water. He took the temporal thought in her mind and turned it into a spiritual application: "Whosoever drinketh of this water shall thirst again: But whosoever drinketh of the water that I shall give him shall never thirst; but the water that I shall give him shall be in him a well of water springing up into everlasting life" (Jn 4:13-14).

An important religious ruler of the Jews named Nicodemus came to see Jesus one night. When he could not understand the teaching concerning being born again of the Spirit of God, Jesus likened the new birth by the Spirit to "the wind [which] bloweth where it listeth, and thou hearest the sound thereof, but canst not tell whence it cometh, and whither it goeth" (Jn 3:8).

The people gathered around Jesus the day after He had fed 5,000 of them with a few loaves and fishes, asking a sign of Him that they might believe! They reminded Him how their forefathers had been given manna from heaven to eat in the desert. Jesus, having just the day before given them such a physical manifestation, gave them a spiritual application: "I am the bread of life: he that cometh to me shall never hunger; and he that believeth on me shall never thirst" (Jn 6:35).

In a land full of vineyards, Jesus said, "I am the vine, ye are the branches: He that abideth in me, and I in him, the same bringeth forth much fruit: for without me ye can do nothing" (Jn 15:5).

Jesus healed the people of their many diseases and afflictions not only to ease their suffering, but also to teach things from the spiritual realm. When a paralyzed man was laid at His feet, Jesus first said to him, "Thy sins be forgiven thee." Then to prove to the Pharisees that He had the power to forgive the man's sins, He told the man, "Arise, take up thy bed, and go unto thine house" (Mt 9:2-6).

When He healed a blind man He said, "For judgment I am come into this world, that they which see not might see; and that they which see might be made blind" (Jn 9:39). He was speaking at the time to the Pharisees who claimed they understood spiritual things. He used the cure of the blind man to illustrate how God gives spiritual sight and understanding to those who truly want them. Jesus illustrated spiritual truths with the weather, water, and wind; food, vegetation, and flowers; fish, birds, animals, and people; the sea, mountains, trees, and fields; precious stones, fire, soil, life, and death; and many other things in creation.

In the Old Testament, God's prophets used physical and material things and demonstrations to get spiritual and prophetical messages across to their people. Moses and Aaron, by their awe-inspiring demonstrations in Egypt through God's power, not only convinced their own people that they had been chosen to lead them out of Egypt and bondage, but also convinced the Egyptians of the mighty omnipotence of their God.

God, in visions and dreams to Joseph, the pharaoh of Egypt, Ezekiel, King Nebuchadnezzar, Peter, and John used animals and vegetation to convey certain prophetic messages. His communication to Jonah came through a little stronger than a dream: Jonah had to be swallowed by a big fish before he obeyed the message!

In Hosea's case, he had to act out with his very life a telling rebuke to God's people, reminding them of God's love for them in spite of their unfaithfulness. Hosea was asked of God to marry a bad woman, and his children were given names symbolic of God's dealing with His people. Lastly he was sent to buy back, to redeem, his unfaithful wife from the slave market where her sinful life had brought her.

The rituals and tabernacle that God gave to the Israelites in the wilderness, as well as the Passover time in Egypt, pictured beautifully the coming of

God's Passover Lamb in the flesh, Jesus Christ. The shedding of blood of sacrificial animals during the Passover and sacrificial rites were physical reminders to the Jews that "without shedding of blood is no remission [of sins]" (Heb 9:22). These were to have prepared them for the time when "the Lamb without spot and blemish" would shed His blood for the sins of the world on the cross.

> And every priest standeth daily ministering and offering oftentimes the same sacrifices, which can never take away sins: but this man, after he had offered one sacrifice for sins for ever, sat down on the right hand of God (Heb 10:11-12).

In order to enter the tabernacle the Jew first had to pass by the sacrificial altar where blood sacrifice for sin was made. After that was a laver where hands and feet were washed, symbolizing how that after we receive Christ as our Saviour, we need to cleanse ourselves with the water of God's Word. Then in the holy place were the shewbread, symbolic of Jesus, the bread of life and our Sustainer; and the lampstand, symbolic of Jesus our light.

In the Holiest of Holies stood the Mercy Seat, symbolic of God's grace. Into this place the high priest entered but once a year to bring the blood offering for sin. When Christ was crucified on the cross, the veil between the holy place and the Holiest of Holies was split, thus symbolizing the free access and entrance of all to God's grace and salvation through the blood of His Son.

There are many other places in the Bible where God uses the material to help us understand the spiritual.

Others of them will be used in the following chapters to illustrate the specific subject being considered. May these precious truths seen in His visible manifestations help you to have a keener understanding of our invisible Creator.

2

THE UNIVERSE

> Praise ye him, sun and moon: priase him, all ye
> stars of light. Praise him, ye heavens of heavens,
> and ye waters that be above the heavens. Let
> them praise the name of the LORD: for he com-
> manded, and they were created. He hath also
> stablished them for ever and ever: he hath made
> a decree which shall not pass (Ps 148:3-6).

CHAOS! Scintillating stars soaring through space crash into each other! Little dark worlds make their dreary, unpurposeful ways through the vast void until at last they fall exhausted into great flaming suns. Nothing about the entire wild scene makes sense. No place in it is a calm place for life to start. For there is no Creator, no intelligence behind it. There is no law, for there is no lawmaker. It is evolution!

Order! Working as perfectly and orderly as an intricate watch, billions of planets, stars, and galaxies wheel and revolve through space perfectly without colliding. Astronomers gaze through their powerful telescopes at stars that sent out the light they are seeing thousands of years ago! Yet every night the same star is in a predictable spot in the universe. Every night the moon is in its place; every day the sun is where it ought to be. In over 3,000 years of astronomical observations, day and night on earth have continued faithfully and on schedule. This is God's creation.

The supreme discovery of science is the orderliness of the universe—in everything from the atom to the galaxy. Astronaut John Glenn states that the orderliness of the vast universe about us is definite evidence that God put it all into orbit and keeps it that way. He said that it just could not be an accident. That is precisely what it all would be without a Creator.

The Vastness of the Universe

Our little earth is just part of a solar system which is part of a galaxy we call the Milky Way. In this galaxy of ours alone there are a hundred billion stars! And there are over a billion more such galaxies in the universe! The vastness of the universe we live in is almost inconceivable to the human mind. Yet the spectroscope, by measuring light from many spiral nebulae and comparing it with our sun, has proved that the entire universe is one, made throughout of the same basic substances!

Our galaxy is not only shaped like a cartwheel, but also the whole gigantic group of which it consists moves like a cartwheel. It is thought to be part of a cluster of galaxies, each galaxy in the group being millions of light years away from the others! Our sun requires two million centuries just to make one circuit around our galaxy. Even within this galaxy the nearest star to earth (besides the sun) is an estimated 25 million of millions miles away. It would take a jet plane six million years to fly that distance.

STARS

> When I consider thy heavens, the work of thy fingers, the moon and the stars, which thou hast ordained; what is man, that thou art mindful of him? And the son of man, that thou visitest him? (Ps 8:3-4).

The average star is a million times larger than our earth. Yet what appears to be one star to the naked eye may be several thousand stars clustered together! Although more than 1,500 million stars have been seen and photographed by astronomers, the heavens are actually far more filled with space than with stars. In fact, at least 99 percent of the universe is nothing but space!

All stars are true suns like our sun, but since the nearest neighboring star to our sun is 250 thousand times farther away from earth, "Old Sol" is the one that predominates in our sky. God gave us just the right sun too, for many stars are much more luminous than our sun and would quickly burn the earth to a crisp if they were as near as our sun. Neither are all stars as stable and steady as our sun, but some flare up and die down. Others fluctuate on longer cycles.

OUR SOLAR SYSTEM

> To him that by wisdom made the heavens. . . . To him that stretched out the earth above the waters. . . . To him that made great lights. . . . the sun to rule by day. . . the moon and stars to rule by night (Ps 136:5-9).

Our solar system may well be the only one in the universe, as there is no proof of any others, and most planetary bodies are either too hot or too cold to sustain life. In the solar system that revolves around our sun, there are nine planets; our earth is the third one from the sun. It is the ideal distance from the sun for the thriving of life, and the perfect size. The sun itself is 700 times more massive than the rest of the solar system combined and is thus able to exert the main gravitational pull on the other bodies in the group.

Gravitation is the force that governs the movements of everything in the universe. This law of nature was discovered by Newton less than 300 years ago. It is gravitation that keeps the planets revolving in orderly fashion around the sun. It makes of our earth a huge magnetic ball, thus holding us and everything else in its retentive protective grip. Who put the law of gravitation into effect in the entire universe? This phenomenon could scarcely have been an accident of nature!

Another thing that plays a factor in the orderly movement of the planets around the sun is that they orbit at just the right speed to continue in their constant movement and position in relation to the sun. Who put these in motion at just the right speed? Someone who is greater than the finest watchmaker in the world did it.

The sun provides us with heat, light, power, beneficial rays, and an orbital hub. Traveling through bitterest cold some 93 million miles, its heat arrives on earth at just the right temperature to warm us. Although its amazing solar engine room keeps putting out fantastic amounts of heat constantly, it has remained practically the same size and strength for the last 500 million years, according to geologists.* It is a self-regulating furnace made by the finest Craftsman that ever existed.

Without the sun all life would quickly disappear from the earth. Plants would not perform their photosynthetic processes, without which both they and animal life would die. For the sun is the source of all energy for life, working through the food chain which starts with green plants. The earth would also become a frozen waste.

The other planets in our solar system are either too far from the sun or too near to it to be actually comfortable for living. But not only would they be uncomfortably hot or cold, but also they apparently are hopelessly too hot or too cold. Further, as far as astronomers can tell, the atmosphere, the gravity, the orbit, or the lack of water on the other planets makes life on them an impossibility. God put life and man on the only planet in this solar system that could sustain them. And earth does that in a marvelous fashion.

The moons that revolve around the other planets are just as dead and lifeless as ours. Some of them revolve in one direction, some in another; yet the solar system works perfectly with no collisions of moons or planets.

If our moon were larger or closer to us, tides would continually wreck our harbors and submerge our

---

*This does not reflect the author's belief in the age of the universe, but is merely a statement of what geologists in general believe.

coastal plains. If it were farther away and smaller, the tides would not be strong enough to cleanse our harbors or rejuvenate the waters of our oceans. The ocean breakers which are caused by the tides provide the life in the sea with oxygen by aerating the water. Thus our moon plays an integral part in life on our earth and was put near our earth by God in His infinite wisdom.

GOD'S GLOBE-SHAPED GREENHOUSE

> Ah Lord God! Behold, thou hast made the heaven and the earth by thy great power and stretched out arm, and there is nothing too hard for thee (Jer 32:17).

For untold centuries civilized men of Europe and Asia firmly believed the earth was flat and that if the ships sailed too far they would sail off the edge! But hundreds of years before Christ was born, a prophet spoke by inspiration of God and told of the true shape of the earth. Isaiah wrote:

> Have ye not known? Have ye not heard? Hath it not been told you from the beginning? Have ye not understood from the foundations of the earth? It is he that sitteth upon the circle of the earth, and the inhabitants thereof are as grasshoppers; that stretcheth out the heavens as a curtain, and spreadeth them out as a tent to dwell in (Is 40:21-22).

Civilized Greeks and Romans also believed that the earth rested on the back of a huge turtle or some god. But the oldest book in the Bible was even then in complete accord with the findings of modern science:

"He stretcheth out the north over the empty place, and hangeth the earth upon nothing" (Job 26:7).

Another popular belief for many years was that the earth was the center of the universe and that the sun revolved around the earth. Yet God said in this oldest book of the Bible:

> Hast thou commanded the morning since thy days; and caused the dayspring to know his place; that it might take hold of the ends of the earth, that the wicked might be shaken out of it? It is turned as clay to the seal (Job 38:12-14).

Because Columbus believed these teachings of the Bible, he discovered America! And there would have been a great many things that man would have known far sooner about the earth and the universe if he had sought the Word of God. This is still true today, for God is eternal and His wisdom is absolute.

We tend to take our earth for granted, its dependability and its wonderful living conditions. Century after century it has faithfully revolved on its axis every twenty-four hours. Once a year, like clockwork, we travel around the sun and cover 584 million miles annually, never varying. We have absolute faith in the laws of the universe, that they will keep us safely. We know that night and day will come, summer, winter, spring, and fall.

Why is it hard for us to have absolute faith in the One who made it so? Because we cannot see Him? Ah, but is not the evidence of His work overwhelming? If He could do all this, can He not also keep His hand on everything that comes into our lives? "The day is thine, the night also is thine: thou hast prepared the light and the sun. Thou hast set all the borders of the earth: thou hast made summer and winter" (Ps 74:16-17).

The earth rotates at exactly the right speed to provide the correct length of day and night for organic life, as we know it, to live. Astronomers agree that the earth is the only planet in our solar system with atmosphere, diameter, mass, position from the sun, rotation, revolution, cycles, balances, and laws capable of maintaining organic life. The earth also is surrounded by a magnetic field which protects all living creatures on earth from powerful cosmic radiation which could produce rapid genetic changes, and could even be deadly. What divine provision!

What a marvelous storehouse our earth is: a veritable paradise full of good things! Just beneath its surface lies its treasure trove of coal, oil, natural gas, iron, aluminum, copper, gold, silver, and precious stones. In its glaciers, oceans, seas, lakes, springs, and rivers resides a vast supply of water that supplies the needs of life. Its surface is covered with abundant verdure of every kind to gladden and satisfy the hearts of man and beast. Its beauty and magnificence are breathtaking. Its atmosphere is a perfect balance of various gases that make earth just right for the existence of human life.

The atmosphere helps to protect us from the harmful ultraviolet rays of the sun and shields us from the barrage of meteors from outer space. It provides an insulation blanket against the extreme cold and heat in space. It diffuses an illuminating glow at night, as well as during the day. How beautiful the Lord made it! Oh, His wonderful sunrises and sunsets! With its particles of dust the atmosphere makes possible the formation of raindrops, snow, and hail which not only distribute water all over the world but also wash valuable substances down to the soil for its fertilization.

Truly the earth is a well-balanced and self-rejuvenating system. All of its plant and animal life are interdependent. God has regulated their growth and multiplication through a fine system of mutual aid and counterbalance. Plants and animals work together for the welfare of each other. Plants take the elements from air and soil and convert them into forms that man and animal can use for their own supply of necessary elements. Animal life helps in the fertilization of plants; their deposits return to the soil the proteins which through decay and soil bacteria ultimately become rich nitrates for them.

Living things are held in check by the "natural enemy" system. The law of conservation of matter set into action by our Father in heaven assures that when anything dies or is burned, it either replenishes the soil or atmosphere. "O LORD, how manifold are thy works! In wisdom hast thou made them all: the earth is full of thy riches" (Ps 104:24).

ALL THINGS BY HIM

God. . . hath in these last days spoken unto us by his Son, whom he hath appointed heir of all things, by whom also he made the worlds. For by him were all things created, that are in heaven, and that are in earth, visible and invisible, whether they be thrones,

> or dominions, or principalities, or powers: all things were created by him, and for him: and he is before all things, and by him all things consist. He was in the world, and the world was made by him, and the world knew him not (Heb 1:1-2, Col 1:16-17; Jn 1:10).

All things were created by the master Creator, God. The Bible also teaches they were made through God's Son. In these verses we see the Godhead in all its glory. How can we separate God? Yet the first verse says that God made the worlds; the next two say that all things were created by God's Son. They are not contrary if you believe in the biblical teaching of the holy Trinity: God the Father, God the Son, and God the Holy Spirit. It is a wonderful truth evident in creation.

Colossians 1:17 says that by God's Son all things consist, that is, hold together. Have not we seen the marvelous truth that this entire universe is one, and working together? Yet again we see that this same One who made all things, and by whom they consist, came into the world and was rejected by the world. It is sad to realize that the Creator of this vast universe actually came to earth in the form of a man and was rejected by His own creatures. Yet it was in that very thing that He was able to win the victory over sin and reconcile His people to Himself through His atonement for their sins. The price of death had to be paid for our sins; and in order that we might have eternal life, God the Son paid for it with His sinless blood. "For God so loved the world that he gave his only begotten Son, that whosoever believeth in him should not perish, but have everlasting life" (Jn 3:16).

The rejection of God's Son still goes on in the world today. Men have the open Bible, they can read God's Word, they can hear it over the radio and television, they can hear it in churches. But in spite of having every opportunity to know what God's Son did for them, they reject Him and His sacrifice. I often wonder why it is that even many ministers and theological students do not believe in the blood atonement of God the Son for their sins. The answer must be that they do not believe the Bible's plain teachings; for if they did, they would believe in His atonement.

It is not necessary for a person to come to the Bible in faith that it is God's Word in order for him to find the truth. Many people do not believe it is God's Word when they first begin their study of it. God's Word does its work regardless of what a person believes about it. The important thing is that a person come to God with a seeking heart, truly and humbly desiring to know the true way, and exposing himself to the Word of God, whether he believes in it or not, for:

> Faith cometh by hearing, and hearing by the word of God. For the word of God is quick, and powerful, and sharper than any two-edged sword, piercing even to the dividing asunder of soul and spirit, and of the joints and marrow, and is a discerner of the thoughts and intents of the heart (Ro 10:17; Heb 4:12).

Thus God's Word does its own convincing. As it finds its way into a person's heart, it reveals the truth of God to him. When a former evolutionist accepted Jesus Christ as his Saviour after his study of the Bible, he acknowledged, "Now I know that this is really God's Word—from cover to cover!"

As we see God in all of His great creation, may we find Him in a personal way through the Word He has given us, and through His Son, Jesus Christ.

3

LITTLE THINGS

> And the LORD God formed man of the dust of
> the ground, and breathed into his nostrils
> the breath of life; and man became a living
> soul (Gen 2:7).

DUST. It seems incredible that such a complex creature as man could have been made of dust. But it is true. Science has discovered that the elements which compose the soil of our world are also the elements found in the makeup of man. But how did these elements get together to form such an intricate being as man? And when they were assembled, who gave them life and intelligence? God.

Besides the fact that the soil of our earth is composed of dust, our atmosphere also is composed of a lighter quantity of dust. Without dust in the air there would be no pretty blue sky, but it would be here as on the moon: black all around us with a bright yellow sun starkly glaring down. If the particles of dust in the air were of a different size, or denser, the sky would be red all the time! Can you imagine how hard that would be on our nerves? When the sun sinks below the horizon its rays have to travel through more atmospheric dust to reach us. The colors in the sky change and reflect the multitude of colors that are really sent out by the sun's rays. Thus we enjoy the exquisite treat of a sunset.

Of what is the dust composed? It contains just about every substance found on our earth: soot, pollen, bacteria, wood, mold, sand, soil, carbon, fine hair, pieces of fiber, thousands of things. Some of it is visible; much of it is microscopic. Some of it is alive; a lot of it is lifeless. In the things of which dust is composed we can find every tiny thing of which our world is composed. Suppose we look into some of these interesting "little things."

Molecules

Molecules are the tiny particles of which almost all matter on earth is composed. A quarter-ounce teaspoon of water contains trillions of molecules. Someone has said, "If the molecules in one drop of water could be converted into grains of sand, there would be enough sand to build a concrete highway a half-mile wide and one-foot thick from New York to San Francisco." The molecules in turn are divided into atoms.

Atoms

Atoms are composed of three essential components: electrons, neutrons, and protons. In spite of having these components in such an infinitesimal unit, there is actually much more space in an atom than there is matter! While molecules are quite a bit similar to galaxies in their constitution, an atom may be compared to our solar system. Electrons dash around the nucleus of an atom millions of times a second, yet they move in orderly fashion.

Mankind, in its search for power, has found the most tremendous source of power through splitting the submicroscopic atom. Scientists worked many years to discover the secret of how to do this. The most intelligent men of our age have worked on the problem. We honor them for their almost unbelievable discovery. But what of the One who put so much potential power in the tiny invisible atom? What of the One who composed all things with the atom? The Bible says: "Through faith we understand that the worlds were framed by the word of God, so that things which are seen were not made of things which do appear" (Heb 11:3).

Protein Molecules

There are over 100,000 different kinds of proteins in the human body which serve a multitude of purposes; these tiny complicated structures are prerequisite for life. Although scientists have been striving for years to create life from lifeless matter or elements, they have yet to succeed. Life itself is something that far transcends the protein molecule!

Viruses

The most primitive of living things, viruses are ultramicroscopic parasites which were never known to have existed until their discovery in recent times. Viruses are the complex structural and chemical entities that are responsible for more than 300 diseases that afflict man, animal, and plant life. Unfortunately it takes just about twenty-four minutes for these little scourges to reproduce themselves 200 times! A virus, which needs to be magnified 100,000 times in order to be seen, has about 150 amino acids in it!

In spite of their rapid rate of multiplication, viruses have never been found to evolve from one species to another. The yellow fever virus has never evolved into a smallpox virus. Through millions of generations it has remained the same pesky critter! If God created the earth and everything in it, why did He create such horrible little creatures that do so much harm? Or did He create them originally that way? Perhaps the answer lies in Romans:

> For the earnest expectation of the creature waiteth for the manifestation of the sons of God. . . . Because the creature itself also shall be delivered from the bondage of corruption into the glorious liberty of the children of God. For we know that the whole creation groaneth and travaileth in pain together until now (8:19-22).

It was not in the plan of God that this should be true for His creation. Nor was it in His plan that man, beasts, or plants should be as predatory or harmful as they are. But the entrance of sin brought its awful penalties: disease, crime, and death. Someday when Satan and his demons and death are cast into the lake of fire by the Almighty God, all the terrible things on earth today will be done away with.

Bacteria

Without bacteria there would be no life on earth, nothing to eat or drink, no vegetation. Bacteria teem in air and water and in the bodies of every living creature. They are microscopic, one-celled plants in a great variety of forms. They range in size from one/ten-thousandth of an inch to one/fifty-thousandth of an inch in diameter and have amazing ability to live and multiply. Many bacteria live on dead matter or as parasites in the bodies of plants or animals. Their chief function is to decompose the dead—leaves, carcasses, plants—thus returning the matter with its rich chemicals to the soil from whence it came.

In breaking down the tissues of dead vegetation, bacteria restore to the air the carbon dioxide so necessary to the life of plants. The plants, in turn, with a goodly supply of carbon dioxide, are able to restore oxygen to the air which is so necessary to the life of animals and men. Without bacteria the supply of carbon dioxide and oxygen would have been exhausted ages ago, and animal and plant life would have ceased to exist. Who can dare to say this amazing balance in nature came about only by pure chance? Surely God, in His infinite providence, created the tiny bacteria!

Bacteria are useful in a number of ways. Some of them live in intestinal tracts and aid in the digestion of food. Some of them form partnerships with plants to supply them with nitrogen. Through the heat which bacteria give to compost heaps, many creatures are perpetuated because that is how their eggs are incubated! Bacteria sour milk for making butter and cheese; they help convert fruit juice into vinegar; they aid in making linen from flax; they are necessary to farmers for making cattle ensilage; and they are necessary to the tanning industry.

Protozoa

There are more than 15,000 species of protozoa, each distinctive from the others. In all of men's experiments with these fast-reproducing organisms, each species constantly remains within the framework of its own kind. Minute, one-celled animals assimilate food, throw off waste products, and reproduce.

The amoeba is perhaps the best-known protozoon. It can breathe, crawl, distinguish that on which it feeds, digest its food. It has no eyes but is sensitive to light; it has no nerve endings but moves away from objects with which it comes into contact. The largest type of amoeba is visible as a tiny white speck, yet the gelatinous protoplasm from which it is made contains many granules and droplets. Although amoebas multiply rapidly, scientists have observed no real change in them through countless generations.

Paramecia are the fast-steppers in the protozoon world. They move quickly about by the means of hairlike cilia which cover the entire cell. These one-cellers are composed of at least eleven different structures! Paramecia have a defensive mechanism that gives them a bristly appearance when they are about to be attacked by some other organism. They reproduce by fission.

Vast numbers of protozoa dwell in the stomachs of cattle. As the protozoa break down the cellulose in the plants on which cattle feed, the cows are able to use the valuable nutritive elements contained in the cellulose. Protozoa also provide one of the major sources of food for fish.

Cells

All living things are made of cells. Bacteria and protozoa are made of only one cell. Man is composed of millions of amazingly varied and intricate cells. Every cell is capable of digestion, absorption, assimilation, excretion, secretion, respiration, motion, sensitivity, and reproduction. Cells divide regularly to add to existing tissues and replace injured or worn-out cells. Each new cell is usually an exact replica of the original cell.

The nucleus of a cell contains chromosomes made up of many vital chemicals, which in turn carry the genes that determine heredity. As microscopic as these chromosomes are, one of man's reproductive chromosomes contains around 30,000 genes, the seeds of inheritance. The number of chromosomes is always the same for a given species and varies all the way from one for protozoa, two for some worms, and several hundred for some animals. Man has forty-six in each cell.

Instead of having forty-six chromosomes like ordinary cells, the sex cells of human beings contain twenty-three chromosomes, so that when the male and female sex cells combine they total the conventional forty-six. This is also true of the animal world. Although cells usually reproduce themselves exactly (i. e., lung cells reproduce lung cells, etc.), an interesting digression is that the original fertilized ovum does not reproduce a like cell. Rather, it goes through an intricate series of divisions and development to become a human being, a fish, a kitten, or some other creature, depending on the parents.

The method of cell reproduction by dividing the chromosomes and re-creating identically assures the stability of a species. However, due to the almost limitless combinations of genes from both parents in animal and plant life, there are no two of any species ever exactly alike. This is why such variety within species is possible. Since the number, kind, and assortment of chromosomes vary with each species of life, and yet do not as a rule vary from generation to generation, therefore it would seem to be a genetic impossibility for one "kind" to ever cross the barrier to another, even though the genes permit such a great variety within the Genesis "kind." Whenever scientists have tried to create mutation in genes with radiation, they have often produced degenerates.

Although man begins life from just one cell, by the time he is born his body has a multitude of specialized cells: gland cells, which produce certain needed substances; fat cells, which store chemicals; bone cells; blood cells; nerve cells; and many others. When these cells die, they are carried out by the bloodstream and replaced with cells like the ones that died.

The Testimony of Little Things

The intricate composition of all these little things and the vital work performed by most of them testify as clearly of God's workmanship as a ship constructed in a bottle testifies of a master craftsman. If this phase of God's creation were to be tested fairly in a court of law, the evidence in favor of the most intelligent Creator that ever lived would overwhelmingly throw any other opinion out of court.

Why will not mankind give as much consideration to the evidence in creation as they will to the facts in a case of litigation? Until a person gives his heart to the Lord, he is usually blind to the truth before his eyes!

The Elements Shall Melt

> And I will shew wonders in the heavens and in the earth, blood, and fire, and pillars of smoke. The sun shall be turned into darkness, and the moon into blood, before the great and the terrible day of the LORD come. But the day of the Lord will come as a thief in the night; in the which the heavens shall pass away with a great noise, and the elements shall melt with fervent heat, the earth also and the works that are therein shall be burned up (Joel 2:30-31; 2 Pe 3:10).

Since men have discovered how to split the atom and release its deadly forces, these verses in the Bible carry ominous portent. If men can split the atom, how much more so can God? If the thought of an atomic war that would cause a chain reaction in the atmosphere brings dread to the hearts of men, how much more then should this prophetic picture of God's judgment on the world strike terror and bring the fear of God to them!

When these prophecies were written, and even up to the present generation, it has probably been hard for people to grasp just what they referred to when they said "pillars of smoke" and "the elements shall melt with fervent heat." Now that we know what the atomic bomb is and can do, we stand in awe that such things were even thought of by prophets of old. But the Bible says: "For the prophecy came not in old time by the will of man: but holy men of God spake as they were moved by the Holy Ghost" (2 Pe 1:21).

The stage may be being set for the great and terrible Day of the Lord. The prophesied confederation of European states and the great world church are in the making today. Israel has once again become a nation, as prophesied. Russia (Gog and Magog) has gained ascendency as a world power, as prophesied. The nations of the Far East are fast becoming powers to be reckoned with, just as prophesied for the last days. The prophecies in the Book of Revelation are about to come to pass, perhaps even in this generation.

Only one escape from the holocaust and judgment to come is offered: "Believe on the Lord Jesus Christ, and thou shalt be saved" (Ac 16:31). 1 Thessalonians 5:9-11 also says:

> For God hath not appointed us to wrath, but to obtain salvation by our Lord Jesus Christ, who died for us, that, whether we wake or sleep, we should live together with him. Wherefore comfort yourselves together.

The comfort of a Christian comes not only from the fact that he does not fear death, but also because he does not face the awful judgment of God coming on all the earth. Revelation 6:12-17 predicts:

> And I beheld when he had opened the sixth seal, and,

lo, there was a great earthquake; and the sun became black as sackcloth of hair, and the moon became as blood; and the stars of heaven fell unto the earth, even as a fig tree casteth her untimely figs, when she is shaken of a mighty wind. And the heaven departed as a scroll when it is rolled together; and every mountain and island were moved out of their places. And the kings of the earth, and the great men, and the rich men, and the chief captains, and the mighty men, and every bondman, and every free man, hid themselves in the dens and in the rocks of the mountains; and said to the mountains and rocks, Fall on us, and hide us from the face of him that sitteth on the throne, and from the wrath of the Lamb: for the great day of his wrath is come; and who shall be able to stand?

There is a far better refuge for men today than fall-out shelters, and that is the Lord Jesus Christ. The fall-out shelters will not prove adequate in that day, but Jesus Christ will have caught all who belong to Him up in the air with Him before that day comes.

4

THE MIGHTY SEA

> In the beginning God created the heaven and the earth. And the earth was without form, and void; and darkness was upon the face of the deep. And the Spirit of God moved upon the face of the waters. And God said, Let the waters under the heaven be gathered together unto one place, and let the dry land appear: and it was so ... and the gathering together of the waters called he Seas; and God saw that it was good (Gen 1:1-2; 9-10).

HERE, IN ALL GOD'S UNIVERSE, is a strange and wonderful thing! In a universe where liquid water is a rarity, here is a world covered by liquid water. What is the meaning of it? What different and unique purpose is this place to serve in God's universe? Ah, now God is parting the waters and putting them into deep reservoirs. "He gathereth the waters of the sea together as an heap: he layeth up the depth in storehouses" (Ps 33:7).

Dry land and mountains rise out of the seas at His command. "The sea is his, and he made it: and his hands formed the dry land" (Ps 95:5). God speaks again, and trees and plants of all kinds spring up. He speaks again, and living creatures of all kinds come into existence. And on the dry land, in a place called the "Garden of Eden," God brings into being His highest creation on earth: man.

All of these creations of God depend on the liquid water surrounding them for life. By a wonderful law of God, water is lifted by the sun from the sea minus all chemicals. Clouds pushed by winds carry it toward its land destinations. It rains (or snows) fresh upon man, beast, and plant to quench their thirst. Mountains, like huge icehouses, hold the precious snow crystals until they are needed for crops. Springs bubble up in arid lands from underground storage vaults. Rivers and streams that dissect and supply all lands of the earth drain the waters back to the oceans from whence they came in a continuous refreshing cycle that surely had a master Engineer to plan it!

> Thou coveredst [the earth] . . . with the deep as with a garment: the waters stood above the mountains. At thy rebuke they fled; at the voice of thy thunder they hasted away. They go up by the mountains; they go down by the valleys unto the place which thou hast founded for them. Thou hast set a bound that they may not pass over; that they turn not again to cover the earth. He sendeth the springs into the valleys, which run among the hills. They give drink to every beast of the field: the wild asses quench their thirst. By them shall the fowls of the heaven have their habitation, which sing among the branches. He

watereth the hills from his chambers: the earth is satisfied with the fruit of thy works. He causeth the grass to grow for the cattle, and the herb for the service of man: that he may bring forth food out of the earth (Ps 104:6-14).

THE MIGHTY POWER OF THE SEA

The surf of the Pacific Ocean thunders against the rocky shoreline. As we watch the foamy spray fly into the air and fall back into the sea, as we hear this thundering roar of the sea, our hearts are filled with awe at its magnificence and power. Those white-crested waves have a story all their own to tell of a trip a thousand miles or more long, which they end before our eyes.

Who can measure the mighty power of the sea? Who can stand against it? Waves and breakers have been known to be as high as sixty feet. Off the northern coast of California a wave 196 feet high stopped the revolving light of a lighthouse there. Thomas Stevenson, the father of Robert Louis Stevenson, developed a wave dynamometer and discovered the force of a wave could be as great as 6,000 pounds per square foot. Piers weighing thousands of tons have been carried away by waves during a storm. What then holds the sea within its certain boundaries? What keeps it from quickly dissolving the rocky shores of our coasts or from constantly conquering the sandy beaches? God says:

> Who shut up the sea with doors, when it brake forth. . . ? [Where wast thou] when I made the cloud the garment thereof, and thick darkness a swaddling-

band for it, and brake up for it my decreed place, and set bars and doors, and said, Hitherto shalt thou come, but no further: and here shall thy proud waves be stayed? Who hath divided a watercourse for the overflowing of waters? (Job 38:8-11, 25).

Yes, God thought of everything when He prepared this home for mankind. His evaporation system, His protective cloud system, His plumbing system, His air-conditioning system, His waterworks system are just perfect. They have served mankind faithfully for thousands of years without breaking down!

Why the Currents and the Tides?

Another system is just as marvelous as those mentioned—the current system God gave the sea through wind, weather, and the rotation of the earth. The climates and the weather around the world are vitally influenced and stabilized by the currents of the sea. Unbearably harsh extremes of temperature would afflict the earth and man were it not for the ocean currents. These currents move cold water toward the equator and warm water toward the poles. By so doing, they not only provide greater areas for the thriving of sea life, but also they are influential in warming or cooling the coasts with which they come in contact. For instance, the current along the western coast of North America has much to do with its temperate climate. On the other hand, the Gulf Stream keeps much of Europe from being unbearably frigid.

The meeting of opposing water masses causes turbulent upswellings of deep, cold, and rich waters. The rich, cold water proves to be an incentive to planktonic life, which thrives in it. This in turn provides an abundance of food for large fish, thus increasing and encouraging the population of the sea. In both the Humboldt Current, off the west coast of South America, and the Benguela Current, off the west coast of Africa, the currents draw up cold mineral-laden water from the depths of the sea in this way to provide the fertilizing elements that sustain the great food chains.

Thus God's system of oceanic currents not only makes climatic conditions pleasant for man but also provides him with an abundance of good food close to shore. Have you ever had occasion to enjoy a day of swimming or fishing in the Atlantic or Pacific Ocean? God's currents make this all so enjoyable!

These currents run along the coastlines of continents. Mid-ocean regions, bounded by the currents, could be called "deserts of the sea," for there is little life seen in them. Only in the last fifteen years, with far more intricate instruments than he had in the past, has man been able to delve into the hidden movements of ocean waters. Much is being learned about the currents in the ocean that has never been known before. Currents running in several directions can be found at different levels in the same areas, each with its own volume and speed. Fish in their migrations undoubtedly make use of these currents as "highways." After bucking them for many years, seafaring men finally learned to make use of them for sailing and to avoid them when going in an opposite direction.

Tides caused by the gravitational pull of the moon

and sun also perform a most necessary function in God's economy. Billions of small creatures such as oysters, mussels, and barnacles, which are unable to search out their food, owe their very existence to the tides that sweep it to them.

The breeding of certain other marine life is timed to coincide with the tide and in many cases depends on it. The unusual breeding systems of the grunion fish and Convoluta worm demand that conditions were "laboratory perfect" for them when they began their existence. Of course the God who made them saw that it was so.

THE GREATEST STOREHOUSE ON EARTH

The ocean is the earth's greatest storehouse of minerals as well as food. There are around 50 quadrillion tons of dissolved salts in all the ocean waters on earth. Many of these, such as magnesium, bromine, and salt, are harvested from the sea by man. There is enough gold in the sea to make every human being in the world a millionaire. But man has not yet discovered how to extract it with profit from the bank of the sea.

Iodine is another difficult thing to extract from the ocean, but almost every creature depends on it for life. Seafood provides a rich source of iodine for us human beings. Actually the animals and plants of the sea are better chemists than men, and are able to find and utilize the mineral wealth of the sea to a greater degree of success. Many of the sea creatures utilize the cobalt, nickel, copper, and vanadium for their bodily welfare and existence.

And, of course, the sea is not only a storehouse for

great mineral wealth and for food, but also it is the great reservoir that holds the water so necessary for the life of man. Though millions of men have lived and died on this planet, the water is still there in the reservoir to supply the needs of untold generations to come. It is something men have taken for granted but really should thank their Maker for!

DID LIFE COME FROM THE SEA?

The majority of evolutionists *conjecture* that life *must* have originated in the sea. They *believe* that it *seems probable* that carbon dioxide, sulphur, nitrogen, calcium, potassium, and phosphorus managed to get together *somehow* in some congenial warm sea, and *in some way* acquired the ability to reproduce themselves and begin the evolutionary chain that eventually led to the development of man.

Although scientists have experimented for years in well-equipped laboratories and applied their highly trained minds to the problem, they still have not been able to produce genuine life out of nonliving matter. Therefore, it certainly seems that it takes more blind faith for evolutionists to believe their amazingly imaginative theory of one-in-a-billion-chance evolution than it does for a Christian to believe God's biblical account of creation. Why then do they cling to such a strange theory? Why does it seem to be so widely accepted?

The Bible says that Satan's keynote saying is, "I will be like God." This infection of pride, sin, and disobedience was passed on to mankind in the Garden of

Eden. That is why we have to humble ourselves in order to find God's truth and way of salvation.

The sea is certainly a vast reservoir of life. On its surface float great masses of plankton, microscopic creatures and plants, which provide a major source of food to the creatures that live in the sea. Many of these plant cells and creatures are so tiny that there could be millions of them in just one cup of sea water. The sea creatures range in size from the plankton to mighty whales that weigh many tons. God filled the sea with all kinds of fish, crustacea, mollusks, and mammals to provide mankind with food, clothing, heat, jewelry, and other blessings. Some nations of people exist almost entirely on food from the sea.

Up until about 150 years ago men thought that nothing could live in the deep sea. With the advance of science it has been discovered that multitudes of strange and fantastic creatures, as well as many we are more familiar with, inhabit the deepest floors of the sea. The many and varied inhabitants of the sea and their interesting peculiarities are considered in further detail in a later chapter.

"The Sea Is His, and He Made It" (Ps 95:9)

Since the One who made the sea is omnipotent, it naturally follows that He has power over the sea He made. The psalmist says of God, "Thou rulest the raging of the sea: when the waves thereof arise, thou stillest them" (Ps 89:9).

Again he says, "The Lord on high is mightier than the noise of many waters, yea, than the mighty waves of the sea" (Ps 93:4). In the Old Testament we have the record of God parting the sea so that the children of Israel might cross on dry land and escape the pursuing Egyptians. Moses and the thousands of Israelites who witnessed this great miracle sang this song of praise:

> Thy right hand, O LORD, is become glorious in power. . . . And in the greatness of thine excellency thou hast overthrown them that rose up against thee. . . . And with the blast of thy nostrils the waters were gathered together, the floods stood upright as an heap, and the depths were congealed in the heart of the sea. The enemy said, I will pursue, I will overtake . . . my hand shall destroy them. Thou didst blow with thy wind, the sea covered them: they sank as lead in the mighty waters (Ex 15:6-10).

If the modern critics who deny that God did this miracle were transported somehow into the realm of the saints, they would find themselves not only in argument with God and with Moses on this point, but also with the venerable Isaiah (51:10); the man of God's own heart, David (Ps 78:13); and the great apostle of the New Testament, Paul (1 Co 10:1-2).

The sage in Proverbs speaks of God's enormous power and omnipotence in this way:

> Who hath ascended up into heaven, or descended? Who hath gathered the wind in his fists? Who hath bound the waters in a garment? Who hath established all the ends of the earth? What is his name, and what is his son's name, if thou canst tell? (Pr 30:4).

God's Son, spoken of in this Old Testament verse, is Jesus Christ. Although men may not fully understand this mystery, Jesus Christ is God. The Bible says, "In the beginning was the Word, and the Word was with God, and the Word was God. And the Word was made flesh, and dwelt among us" (Jn 1:1, 14). This passage refers to none other than Jesus Christ, the incarnation of God in the flesh.

Perhaps one of the incidents most revealing of Christ's deity was when He Himself commanded the sea and it obeyed Him, just as it obeyed God in Moses' day. Jesus' disciples came to Him during a terrible storm in which the waves threatened to capsize their ship. They awoke Him from sleep, crying, "Lord, save us: we perish!"

As He turned to look at His frightened disciples, He rebuked them, saying, "Why are ye fearful, O ye of little faith?" Then He arose and rebuked the winds and the sea, and there was a great calm. But the men marveled, saying, "What manner of man is this, that even the winds and the sea obey him!" (Mt 8:24-27).

Let us hear the testimony of a humble fisherman who was present several times when Christ stilled the raging waves of the sea. Simon Peter, would you like to tell us about one of your outstanding memories of Christ?

"Well, I guess one of the greatest experiences I had while with my Lord was the time I tried to walk on the stormy sea of Galilee."

"You mean to say that you actually tried to walk on the sea, Peter? What made you do a thing like that?"

"It happened like this," answers Peter. "Jesus had just finished preaching to a huge crowd of people, as well as healing all the sick people there. He was tired, and He wanted to go alone into the mountain to pray. He told us disciples to take the ship and cross the sea ahead of Him. The stars were out that night and we thought we'd have smooth sailing all the way. But when we got out in the middle, one of those sudden Galilean storms hit us, and we began to have a terrible time controlling the ship!"

"Go on, Peter. What happened then?"

"All at once John yells over the gale, 'Look! There's a ghost walking on the water out there!'

"Then Andrew says, 'You must be seeing things, John. You know there aren't any such things as ghosts!' Then he looks and he turns white.

"I look in the direction they're staring and, sure enough, there in the dark mist is something walking out on the water!

"'It's a spirit!' I cry, with my heart in my throat.

"But a voice comes back, saying, 'Be men of courage! It is I; stop being afraid.' It was the Master's voice!

"So I cry out, 'Lord, if it is You, let me come to You on the water!'

"And He said, 'Come.' With that I climb out of the ship, and there I was, walking on the water!

"But the wind blew against me. A wave dashed waist high. I took my eyes off Jesus and became frightened, and then I began to sink! I could feel the cold, icy-fingered waves closing around me. I cried, 'Lord, save me!'

"Jesus was right next to me then, and He reached out His hand and pulled me up out of the murky waters. 'O you of little faith,' He said. 'Why did you waver so?'

"As we climbed into the boat, the storm ceased. Then we all fell down before Jesus with profound reverence and worshiped Him, saying, 'Truly You are the Son of God!'

"Now honestly, do you think anyone but God in the flesh could do those things?"

The apostle Paul told the people of Lystra, "Turn from these vanities unto the living God, which made heaven, and earth, and the sea, and all things that are therein" (Ac 14:15). This is the same exhortation given by the servants of God today to people everywhere. Indeed, it is the reason why this book was written, in the hope that many might become aware of the hand of God in all creation and turn to Him who made it.

The Bible holds the promise of hope for every person on earth who will turn to God:

> Who is a God like unto thee, that pardoneth iniquity. . . ? He retaineth not his anger for ever, because he delighteth in mercy. He will turn again, he will have compassion upon us; he will subdue our iniquities; and thou wilt cast all their sins into the depths of the sea (Mic 7:18-19).

5

THE PLANT WORLD

> He causeth the grass to grow for the cattle, and herb for the service of man: that he may bring forth food out of the earth; and wine that maketh glad the heart of man, and oil to make his face to shine, and bread which strengtheneth man's heart (Ps 104:14-15).

IT IS MAY IN THE COUNTRY! We are standing at the top of a ridge overlooking a panoramic view of the countryside. Birds are singing and hopping about in the nearby maple tree. The luxurious green grass feels soft beneath our feet. In one field extending down the ridge, tender green shoots of corn stretch themselves sunward. In another field black and white cows graze contentedly. Soon the grass they eat will be turned into rich creamy milk for the use of their owners and townsfolk.

As we turn a bit we see one of the forests that dot this ridge. The trees rustle proudly in their new green apparel. Out of these woods came the timber that made many of the farmhouses, barns, and fences in this area. In the winter the wood is used in big old wood-burning stoves, not only to heat the homes, but also to simmer kettles of soup. In the fall the woods turn into a riot of color. Then when the leaves begin to fall, we will gather the nuts that fall to the ground with them.

On one side of the farmyard is a group of apple trees. We recall with a thrill having enjoyed their abundant array of sweet-smelling blossoms earlier in the spring. In the fall we will enjoy their delightful red and yellow fruits. We slip a crimson strawberry we have just picked into our mouth and savor its delectable tart-sweet flavor. The fields all around are redundant with wild flowers. The farmyard, too, is a picture in color as irises vie with daffodils. Soon velvety dahlias, showy peonies, and fragrant roses will add to the delightful surroundings.

This is God's creation: beauty, color, symmetry, utility. Without the plant world which He created first, no other life could possibly exist on earth. In all the wondrous plant world can be seen the hand of God. "O LORD, how manifold are thy works! In wisdom hast thou made them all: the earth is full of thy riches" (Ps 104:24).

Plants may be as tiny as the microscopic bacteria or as huge and ancient as the mighty Sequoias in California. Many trees soar over 200 feet in height. Some, as old as 4,000 years, may have been saplings in Moses' day. The Ginko, or Maiden Hair Tree, exists in China and Japan the same as it did thousands of years ago.

Algae

Algae serve a vital purpose in God's creation by providing undersea life with oxygen and food. Smaller fish exist almost entirely on algae, and even many larger fish get much of their nourishment from these plants.

Algae range in size from microscopic one-celled plants to gigantic deep-sea kelps. They are often responsible for coloring seas green, turquoise, or red; for not only are they every beautiful color imaginable, but some even scintillate with iridescent hues. Some algae, like the rockweed and gulfweed, are equipped by God with tiny pontoons or air bladders to enable them to float on the water, thus giving them good circulation and keeping them from matting.

The microscopic group is among the host of tiny organisms that form plankton, which is a vital part of the food chain for aquatic creatures. Algae are rich in proteins, vitamins, and other essential nourishing ingredients; thus kelp is considered a valuable additive to the human diet. Algae provide a good fertilizer for man, as well as a material called "agar-agar" which is used by hospitals and laboratories all over the world as a culture media for bacteria.

Fungi

Somewhat comparable to algae, fungi consist of a large group of one-celled or multicelled organisms of which there are about 100,000 species. While some of these parasitic plants seem to cause much mischief, others have proved to be most useful to man. Since ancient times fungi have been used as medicine, and in our world today antibiotics such as penicillin and streptomycin are formed by fungi.

Through decomposition of dead plants, bacteria return to the soil the vital nitrates so necessary to the life of growing things. Bacteria further aid man in the preparation of such basic foods as bread, butter, cheese, and vinegar.

Fungi are also useful for a number of industrial processes. They are used in the production of glue, synthetic resins, inks, dyes, citric acid, industrial ethyl alcohol, commercially usable oils, and cheese. Even Vitamin D, riboflavin, and biotin, which are nutritional helps to man, can be made with the aid of fungi. And something that is a vital part of our daily diet is also made with fungi: bread! Yes, the yeast used to make our bread rise is actually fungi. Bread would not be nearly so tasty, would it, if we did not have these tiny activators to make it rise!

LICHENS

Lichens are actually a combination of two separate plants of different kinds: a fungus and an alga. God has so blended these two together that even when the wind wafts their offspring away to a new place, the two fly away like Siamese twins. Lichens can thrive in places where algae alone or fungi alone could not live. They can exist closer to the poles and to the tops of high mountains than any other plants. They also exist on deserts and rocks. Lichens play an important role in soil formation in rocky regions, and they provide food for cattle and deer in Arctic regions.

Mosses

Mosses, as well as most other plants, are useful and beneficial. They are the first plants able to put roots down in barren places, thereby providing a compost footing for larger plants and trees. Their rhizoids secrete substances that break down rocks gradually and form more soil. They, too, are absolutely necessary to the plant and animal life of our planet.

The mosses provide fuel for many peoples in the form of peat; they are used to dress wounds, for packing and shipping flowers, and other purposes.

Ferns

In ages past God could see into the future when mankind would need coal and oil for fuel and engine power. In preparation for that need thousands of ferns lived and died. Today we have great coal and oil fields which have contributed tremendously to the advance of our modern civilization. We still have the ferns with us and they make our flower bouquets lovely. Even though they seem like very simple plants, they have just as intricate and interesting a reproduction process as most of the flowering plants. How did this reproduction process start? It had to be there in the very beginning of existence of the first fern!

Seed Plants

We have looked briefly at several groups of the plant world. But the group to which the majority of plants belong provides us with some of the most wonderful examples of God's creative hand in the plant world. These are the seed plants—all the plants which produce seeds rather than spores. The seed plants (trees fall into this category) consist of four intricate organs: roots, stems, leaves, and flowers. Consider these wonderfully complex parts one by one:

ROOTS

We look casually at the root of a plant and what do we see? It looks like nothing but some pieces of coarse string, certainly not very complicated. But the roots of a plant serve a twofold purpose. They provide a base, a foundation, or a mooring for the plant, and they collect the life-preserving water and nitrates from the soil for the plant's needs. On the growing tip of each root is a small cap called "calyptra." This cap, moved by cell growth behind it, recoils from obstructions, and finds its way miraculously to water.

More marvelous than a man-made hydroelectric plant, the roots absorb water through a special water-breathing construction and send it coursing up the plant through osmosis. Roots often establish a partnership with soil bacteria, absorbing them to get the vital nitrogen in the soil. A slender root of a tree can split a solid rock.

Mangrove and blackjack trees have a root system especially made for them by God. Since they grow in swamps of mud and water, their tough, stiff roots reach up like stilts to the trunk above. Thus, the flow of water does not weaken one stout trunk, but flows easily among the many strong stilts. These trees with their peculiar roots have added many thousands of acres of fertile land to Florida and other places where they abound. Their offspring stay on the tree until they have sprouted roots, so that when they fall off the parent, they are ready to grab the bottom and anchor themselves firmly. Otherwise they would be swept out to sea. Here again is another thing about nature: if it had had to evolve, it never would have made the grade!

STEMS, TRUNKS, AND LIMBS

Coursing with the lifeblood of sap, the stem or trunk of a plant is honeycombed with miniature canals through which flow the life-giving substances. Progressing downward, nourishment manufactured by the leaves makes its way throughout the tree to the roots. But the most amazing thing is the upward movement of water and nourishment. Every plant is a living hydraulic jack! Hydraulic pressure of the sap keeps the plants erect in heavy winds, helps them grow tall, and enables their roots to break rocks. Plants are hydraulic masterpieces, carrying on their continual struggle with the law of gravity.

Every living cell in a plant is a tiny powerhouse, absorbing water and passing it on. The leaves aid in this struggle too; for as they lose water through evaporation, fresh water seeps into the vacuum left. Root suction, osmosis, and leaf pull all work together like a team of scientists. Even the water cooperates in this upward struggle through cohesion. If we consider mankind's waterworks to be wonderful things and give credit to those who masterminded them, how much more should we give glory to God for the intricate process He built into every tree in existence!

The heartwood or central core of a tree or plant acts as its spine; the bark is its protective insulating cover, like a cuticle; the sap is its nourishing blood. Plants breathe, eat, and drink, and then they turn their food and drink into growth. Has man ever invented anything more wondrous than a plant? If plants require more sunshine, they will twist and turn their trunks and branches in order to get more. God equipped many plants with hairy stems and branches to keep off pilfering ants and beetles.

LEAVES

The leaves are not only the lungs of a plant, but also the stomach! The next time you look at some tiny leaf, just think of the amazing things that go on inside it! Lined with veins for support and the passage of life-giving fluid, a leaf is covered with a thin skin. This skin has pores automatically regulated to control the passage of air and moisture. (How's that for an air-conditioning system?) Some leaves are further protected by hairs, scales, or a coating of wax.

Although a leaf seems paper thin, between its covers the space is filled with mesophyll, made up of protoplasm. The leaf also contains "chloroplasts." These contribute its chlorophyll, a wonderful substance that converts water, air, and sunbeams into living tissue. We have blood; a leaf has chlorophyll.

The simple-appearing leaf is actually an amazing chemical lab more efficient than any operated by man. To do the same job a leaf does, a laboratory needs large, intricate equipment which must use enormous amounts of energy. With matchless efficiency a leaf does what a chemist can equal only by using fiery temperatures and with excessive waste. Utilizing sunbeams, the chloroplasts tear apart carbon dioxide and water molecules, rearranging their atoms to form sugar and oxygen. Sugar for energy, proteins for body, and starch for sustaining life are manufactured by the leaf from the four elements: carbon, nitrogen, oxygen, and hydrogen. Some leaves also produce gums, waxes, oils, fats, acids, alkaloids, scents, and odors. Thus the tiny leaf serves as a laboratory, a manufacturer, and a storage warehouse! God created this marvelously versatile little thing!

The leaf has three vital functions: photosynthesis, transpiration, and respiration. Through photosynthesis it absorbs carbon dioxide and releases great volumes of oxygen and thus purifies and revitalizes air for men. It sifts out just the rays of sunlight that will transform lifeless gas and water into protoplasm. In transpiration it gives off excess moisture (like perspiration), thus cooling the air all around on a hot day. At night, when it is cool, the leaf breathes in necessary oxygen and exhales carbon dioxide, just as animals do in respiration.

Leaves change color in the fall when the chlorophyll diminishes and other pigments that have been present all along then can be seen in their rich hues of red, gold, and orange. The food products in the leaf are transferred to the main body of the tree as the little labs close down for the winter.

When exposed to too much sun, leaves turn their

thin edges to the light. In the gloom they turn their broad sides. The leaves of the chestnut, oak, elm, and beech are arranged on vertical shoots in spirals so that all the leaves can get enough sunlight. Clover, beans, and peas fold their leaves when darkness comes.

PROPAGATION: THE FLOWER'S WORK

What would have been the result if the very first plant of each kind had not been completely equipped for propagation? Surely students of biology know about the intricate and fascinating processes of propagation so necessary for the continuation of many plant species. Many people who have attended high school have studied this interesting subject.

First come the flowers. Flowers have male and female organs; anther and stigma. Some plants produce flowers with both organs; other plants produce flowers with one or the other. In order to produce seeds, the pollen from an anther has to be transferred to a stigma. In many cases a flower is either gorgeously colored or sweetly scented in order to attract an insect or bird to carry its pollen to another flower. Some flowers, however, merely depend upon wind or water to do the job. Still others are self-fertilizing.

Some flowers exude a stronger perfume at the time of day when the particular insects that fertilize them are on the wing. God also made the flowers with special landing strips for their particular pollen carriers. And have you ever noticed the guidelines of contrasting colors that are made into the flowers to lead the insect to the nectar and pollen? Many plants require just a certain species of insect or bird to fertilize them. The magnolia flower has a triggerlike trap that is sprung when the Catonia beetle lights on it. A sudden shower of petals from the flower startles the insect and causes it to take off for another flower laden with the pollen from the first flower. Its back rubs against the stigma of the new flower, and the pollen is deposited right where it needs to be!

The beautiful yucca desert flower depends for its propagation on a tiny white moth that only comes out at night. This moth appears on the very night the yucca blooms and carries a large piece of pollen from one plant to another. Then she lays her eggs nearby, and her babies use the seeds which come from the cross-pollination as their food. There are always enough seeds left, however, to continue the propagation of the yucca flower. Thus the two, plant and insect, work together in a harmony that could only have been conceived in the mind of God. Since their lives are interdependent, their creation had to come simultaneously, or close together at least. There are several species of yucca, and each has its own species of moth and cannot be pollinated by any of the other moths!

The orchid is also very particular as to its propagation. That is why it can only be artificially propagated out of its natural clime. Some orchids bar all insects from entering their gorgeous blossoms, only allowing the beak of the hummingbird to enter. One species of orchid has a mutual-aid agreement with a family of vicious red ants. The ants make their home among its roots and feed on its nectar. In return, they not only fertilize the plant but also protect it. This orchid cannot even bear flowers without the presence of these red ants.

The iris has a drooping stigma which rolls the pollen of another flower off a bee's back as he enters the flower. While the fat, furry little friend is sucking the nectar, he picks up a new load of pollen from the anther. The stigma straightens up, so that when the bee backs out of the flower he carries his new load with him!

Jean Henry Fabre, the Homer of insects, said, "Before these mysteries of life, reason bows and abandons itself to adoration of the Author of these miracles."

PROPAGATION: SEEDS AND FRUIT

Shaped like fishhooks, covered with feathery down, barbed, burred, covered, or winged, seeds are hitchhikers, parachutes, autogiros, or boats, depending on their particular anatomy. Some plants, such as touch-me-nots and pansies, are miniature guns. Their seed pods burst open with a pop and throw seeds some distance. Some, like cherries, are covered with toothsome delights so that birds will carry them far and wide. Some are specially built to float on the sea to far destinations (such as the cocoanut and the Indian mulberry).

Most seeds have a protective covering; those that do not are produced in huge quantities to offset the seeds that do not survive. Within a seed coat is a complete new plant, ready to start growing. Seeds are made by God to endure conditions which would be fatal to the parent plant. Heat, cold, and drought do not injure this well-protected embryo. Until growing conditions are favorable, the seed remains dormant.

It is wonderful how a sprouting seed can find its way to the surface and then penetrate hard-packed earth, lifting soil many times its own weight. What a miracle of life one tiny seed contains! Digestion, absorption, and assimilation actually take place in a seed when it starts to grow.

PROPAGATION: EACH ITS OWN KIND

Hugo de Vries succeeded in obtaining 834 mutations belonging to seven distinct types out of 53,500 plants of the Great Evening Primrose. However, after all was said and done, "a rose is a rose is a rose" is still true. In all these experiments, that rose never became a chrysanthymum, or a berry bush, or a vegetable; it was still an evening primrose.

God's Gifts to Man Through Plants

Plants provide us with almost everything we need to be healthy and happy. From the wood of trees we make our houses and furniture. Wooden ships enabled men to discover America and to sail all over the world. Wooden airplanes first took men into the wide blue yonder. Our great libraries are filled with fine books made entirely from the products of trees and plants.

The Lord has provided us with every type of delectable, tasty food imaginable: fruits, nuts, grains, vegetables, sugars, and spices. Even the meat we eat and the milk we drink are by-products of the insignificant grasses. Certainly our lives are made more enjoyable by the many beverages we concoct from fruits, beans, and leaves.

Textiles, drugs, medicines, beauty aids, perfumes, fuels, rubber, oil, resin, and dyes are just some of the things God has provided us by means of His versatile plants. Plants give us shade, fragrance, beauty, and soil conservation. They also make a home for birds and animals.

Even many of our commonest weeds have some commercial value or possess valuable medicinal qualities. Some weeds are edible, and dyes are made from others. The most undesirable, obnoxious weeds in a land usually prove to be alien weeds, transplanted from their native lands, their natural enemies left behind.

> God's locale for them was best,
> For when at home they weren't a pest.

Some Plant-World Wonders

Practically every need of man can be met by palm trees: food, drink, clothing, medicine, fuel, light, timber, boats, bedding, dishes, nets, twine, and many other things! Some palm trees grow in the deserts at oases and provide men and camels with shade and nutritious food in a barren land. The cocoanut palm lives under the most trying circumstances. It puts its roots down in a sandy seashore and is lashed by hurricane winds. But its leaves are so formed that they offer little resistance to the fierce gale, and its flexible-touch trunk bends and sways without cracking. If the palm is uprooted during a storm, it just regains its hold in the soil with its roots, turns its face toward the sun and grows from the point where it fell.

The Travelers' Palm, a native of Madagascar, has been introduced into many tropical lands because of its drinking-fountain quality. At the base of each of its leaf stems is a trough containing a quart or more of clear, sweet water. A thirsty man can sate his thirst by making an incision where this pocket is. Tropical trees such as baobabs, tefeldi, and silk-cotton serve the natives of many lands as handy "water towers." Water remains in the hollow trunks of these trees and is sweet, pure, and cool indefinitely. Natives in jungles get their emergency drink from liana vines.

The barrel cactus, which lives in desert lands, has a lifesaving supply of water in itself which has quenched the thirst of many a desert man or Indian. When a piece is sliced off its top and a scoop hollowed out, clear, cool water flows into this desert cup.

It is fascinating to note that practically all thirst-quenching plants are located in arid or hot lands. This was certainly not by accident, but in the kind plan of God. Lands that have deserts are also especially provided by God with juicy fruits and vegetables, such as grapes, melons, cucumbers, and pomegranates to implement man's need for liquids.

DESIGN, SYMMETRY, BEAUTY, AND FRAGRANCE

When you see a lovely design in something, have you ever wondered who the clever designer was? In almost every case of a beautiful design, it has been done before, in nature, by God. Everything in the plant world makes an ornament for the eyes to enjoy. Petals, leaves, flowers, and trees are symphonies in symmetry.

Have you ever noticed the symmetrical beauty of the stately elm, the pyramidal spruce, the graceful palm, the gorgeous maple, the shining white birch, the sturdy oak, the feather-soft juniper, the silvery rustling poplar? Look at the leaves of some of these trees and see how they differ from one another in form and design. Yet each one is uniformly perfect according to its species! The gorgeous blossoms of some trees, such as the magnolia, tulip, apple, and cherry, bear further evidence of the hand of God in their creation.

And the magnificent color array in a garden! Rich purples, downy pinks, spotless whites, showy reds, sunshine yellows, dainty blues, flaming oranges, and flowers with several colors, like the grimacing pansies, vie with one another to catch our eyes. This wondrous variation of color and symmetry no more came into being by itself than did Grandma's patchwork quilt!

Have you ever looked closely at the common weed, Queen Anne's lace? If you do so, you will find it a marvel of design, fit to compare with the finest lace tablecloth. Dainty white flowerets form the umbels. Look at each tiny flower; each one is perfect! Each one has five tiny petals, grouped around a tinier center, and there are dozens of these flowerets in every bloom. Usually in the center one can find a single dark purple flower. It is wondrous to find this intricacy of detail in just a weed of the field. Jesus said:

> And why take ye thought for raiment? Consider the lilies of the field, how they grow; they toil not, neither do they spin: and yet I say unto you, That even Solomon in all his glory was not arrayed like one of these. Wherefore, if God so clothe the grass of the field, which to day is, and to morrow is cast into the oven, shall he not much more clothe you, O ye of little faith? (Mt 6:28-30).

All of these: the downy balls of dandelions, the spreading umbels of elder blossoms, the tassels of the currant, the pointed spires of the crane's bill in seed, the stars of the thistle, the velvety nobility of the orchid, the graceful petal canopies of the iris, the dainty perfection of forget-me-nots, the dainty white bells of the lily of the valley with their exquisite fragrance, the snapdragon with its multitude of perfect flowers on one stalk, and the carnations—poetry in ragged petals—say that there is a Creator.

Spiritual Seed-Sowing

When Jesus Christ lived as a man on this earth, He loved to use the things of His creation to illustrate His spiritual teachings. One of His best-known parables concerns the sowing of seeds and the results. The parable is found in both Matthew 13 and Luke 8.

Some of the seeds sown fell by the wayside, and the birds ate them up. Some fell on stony places and sprang up quickly; but with not much root, they soon withered away. Some fell among thorns, and the thorns sprang up and choked them. Other seeds fell on good ground and brought forth much fruit.

And this was Jesus' interpretation of His parable: When someone hears the Word of God and does not understand it, then Satan takes it quickly away, just as the birds ate the seed by the wayside. When someone hears the Word with joy but turns away shortly because he cannot take tribulation or persecution that comes with being a faithful Christian, he is like the stony places on which the seed fell. The person who received the seed among the thorns is one who becomes unfruitful because of the cares of this world and the deceitfulness of riches. The one who receives the seed on good ground is the person who both hears the Word and understands it. He is the one who brings forth fruit.

Have you ever wondered about the difference between Christians? Some Christians seem to radiate with their devotion to Christ; they love to talk about the Lord and His Word. Most professing Christians, however, seem to steer clear of the subject of religion or only talk about it reluctantly. The winning of souls, the "fruit-bearing," is usually done by only a precious few Christians. Many profess to believe in Christ; few want to bear the consequences of witnessing for Him. That is because so few people will allow the ground in their hearts to be tilled and fertilized with the Word of God. The more saturated we become with the Word of God, the easier it is for us to hear and understand it and to put it into practice.

THORNS

Jesus likened thorns to the cares of this world. Of course it is an excellent simile. No doubt you have heard people ask, "Why are there so many troubles in the world: famine, sickness, tragedies, crimes? If there is a God, why does He permit such things? Actually when Adam and Eve committed the first sin against God, they opened a veritable "Pandora's box" filled with the terrible results of sin for themselves and their descendants. This had not been God's wish for man, but man brought it upon himself.

God, being a just God, also had to pronounce certain judgments because of the transgression, just as judges today pass judgments on criminals who transgress man's law. One of the judgments was:

> Because thou hast hearkened unto the voice of thy wife, and hast eaten of the tree, of which I commanded thee, saying, Thou shalt not eat of it: cursed is the ground for thy sake; in sorrow shalt thou eat of it all the days of thy life; thorns also and thistles shall it bring forth to thee (Gen 3:17-18).

This then is how it came about that the world is filled with noxious weeds which seem to have no useful purpose. Because man's transgression lay in the realm of the food department, that is where a curse had to come from as judgment. Just as thorns crowd out good plants and keep them from bearing fruit, so the cares of this world and the deceitfulness of riches crowd out the Word of God from the heart of a person who may have at first received the good news of God's salvation with great joy. How can this be prevented?

In order for good plants to grow, the farmer has to pull out the thorny weeds. Of course it is hard and sometimes painful work, but the resultant fruit proves worth the effort. So the person who at first came to Jesus with great joy, but slid back because of various reasons, needs to uproot those weeds in his heart that keep him from being a fruitful Christian. How? By allowing the Word of God and the Holy Spirit of God free access to his heart and life to uproot those noxious, fruit-killing things: worry, lack of faith, covetousness, worldliness, and other sins.

TARES

According to Jesus, tares are sown among the good seed by the enemy of God, Satan (Mt 13:24-30). These tares are almost indistinguishable from real wheat until fully grown. For that reason they are the most destructive of all weeds to the farmer. The inner coats of tare seeds often harbor seriously poisonous fungus growths that, if eaten by humans or animals, will cause dizziness and vomiting, and sometimes death.

In this case Jesus says "the good seed are the children of the kingdom" (Mt 13:38). Children of the Kingdom of God are those who are born into God's family (born again spiritually) through receiving Jesus Christ as their personal Saviour. They believe that Jesus shed His blood on the cross for their sins. They are "washed in the blood of the lamb" (Col 1:12-14).

The tares, on the other hand, are people who look and sound so much like Christians that they are thought to be Christians. However, they are really children of the devil (just as Jesus said the Pharisees were). These tares are just as harmful and destructive to the Church of Jesus Christ as real tares are among the wheat. If they are not promoting some false doctrine, they are busy causing division in the Church. Since true Christians are imperfect at best, it usually cannot be stated dogmatically who is the tare and who is wheat (Mt 13:29). Thus Jesus says that when harvesttime comes at the end of the world, the tares will be gathered and they will be "cast into a furnace of fire: there shall be wailing and gnashing of teeth" (Mt 13:39-42).

Fruit and Harvest

Jesus spoke of several kinds of harvests: one great harvest at the end of the world at which time the tares will be separated from the wheat; and the continual harvesting of lost souls by Christians into the Kingdom of God.

The time of harvest at the end of the world will be a time of great judgment. God will judge the nations, and He will judge individual people. Each person will be judged depending on whether or not he accepted the sacrifice of God's only begotten Son, Jesus Christ, for his sins (Jn 3:36). If he has not, his portion will be in the lake of fire where the torment will last forever (Rev 20:10-14).

The continual harvesting of lost souls was spoken of by Jesus:

> The harvest truly is great, but the labourers are few: pray ye therefore the Lord of the harvest, that he would send forth labourers into his harvest. Say not ye, There are yet four months, and then cometh harvest? Behold, I say unto you, Lift up your eyes, and look on the fields; for they are white already to harvest. And he that reapeth receiveth wages, and gathereth fruit unto life eternal: that both he that soweth and he that reapeth may rejoice together (Lk 10:2; Jn 4:35-36).

Thus great reward in the life to come is promised to the witnesses and soul-winners for Jesus Christ. And not just those who succeed in leading the soul to Christ, but those who planted and watered the seed will share in the rejoicing and the recompense.

Again using the plant world for illustration, Jesus gave us the conditions under which people may be fruitful witnesses for Him:

> I am the true vine, and my Father is the husbandman. Every branch in me that beareth not fruit he taketh away: and every branch that beareth fruit, he purgeth it, that it may bring forth more fruit. Now are ye clean through the word which I have spoken unto you. Abide in me, and I in you. As the branch cannot bear fruit of itself, except it abide in the vine; no more can ye, except ye abide in me. I am the vine, ye are the branches: He that abideth in me, and I in him, the same bringeth forth much fruit: for without me ye can do nothing (Jn 15:1-5).

Those who are Christians, then, need to be as closely bound to our Lord Jesus Christ as the branch is to the vine in order to bear fruit for Him!

6

INSECTS AND ARACHNIDS

> The ants are a people not strong, yet they prepare their meat in the summer. The locusts have no king, yet go they forth all of them by bands; the spider taketh hold with her hands, and is in kings' palaces (Pr 30:25, 27-28).

HAVE YOU EVER BEEN in the country on a warm summer night and heard the chorus of insects blending their sounds together? It seems as if all the night is filled with happy contented noises, and one drifts into a blissful serenity induced by the soothing symphony. It is more pleasant and restful than the sweetest of man-made music!

Watch the fireflies flicker their fluorescent lights on and off in their unpredictable whirls. It makes one think of ballerinas dancing on a darkened stage with lights on their toes. A sense of almost being lifted out of yourself takes over with the balmy magic of the insect-filled night.

Actually the thought and sight of insects and spiders fills most of us with repulsion. But just as the magic of their sounds and lights brings serenity to the soul, so the magic of their God-given tasks benefits the world of men, animals, and plants. Without the ministrations of the insects, many of the plants we depend on and take for granted would be nonexistent, for they depend on the insects for cross-fertilization. Indeed, many plants depend on one particular insect as their only means of propagation.

Insects also play an important balance in the world of nature. Only 1 percent of the insects are harmful to the interests of men. But even this one percent is used for food by birds and may have some other use in the plan of God that we have not yet discovered. Some insects or their larvae feed on noxious weeds, other insects, or other creatures. Aphids and crickets prefer the larvae of beetles and the roots and stems of weeds for their diets. The dragonflies feast on mosquitoes. And there is a certain small fly that lays its eggs among cutworms, thus cutting down on damage done to cabbage.

The bees extract honey for us from the flowers and also give us wax. The silkworm moth weaves gossamer threads of silk for some of the more luxurious clothing of mankind. The laccifer, of the aphid family, produces shellac. A scaly insect in China produces a very fine, high-melting wax used for candles, for polishing jade, and as a finish on expensive paper. Wasps first taught man how to make paper from wood pulp. Some insects provide man with ink and gorgeous dyes.

Since there are about a million species of insects, we could not possibly look at the evidence of God's creative hand in all of them. So we will settle for a few of the more well-known insects. Even as we take a close look at them, it is hard to believe that such tiny things are capable of doing the amazing things that they do! Consider the ant.

Ants

There are over 2,500 species of ants, each species with three genders: queens, males, and workers. As the queen ant lays her eggs, the workers (undeveloped females) place them in nurseries, moving them about occasionally so that they get the necessary amount of heat and moisture. When the eggs hatch, the workers also take care of the larvae and see that they are fed semidigested food. The worker ants bury the larvae in the ground when they are ready to spin their cocoons and dig them up precisely when the cocoon is finished. They bring them to the nest, and when the feeble young ant is ready to emerge from the cocoon, the workers help to free it.

The ants have a well-organized community life. They gather food, feed their young, and tend to their domestic animals; each ant has its particular task to do. They have well-planned dwelling places, with a central meeting hall. They make numerous entrances to their habitations and have outside roads leading up to their hill. Some of the ants even stand guard duty at night.

Some ants are nursemaids, some are soldiers, and some keep cows (aphids). Some ants make biscuits (out of fermented seeds), and some run farms (raising fungi or rice). Some are city builders, some build tree houses, and some are seamstresses sewing leaves together!

The farmer ants live in South America and actually cultivate gardens. They make their nests in trees. They carry earth in their mouths and mold it into a huge mass which they honeycomb with their living quarters. They turn the outer surface into farms, sowing seeds of various small plants to provide food. The fourteen different plants they grow are never found growing in any other place than on these ants' nests!

The umbrella ants of the American tropics raise mushrooms. They form hotbeds with pellets of tree leaves they have shredded and prepared in their mouths. Then they sow the threads of a fungus which only they possess. They tend, weed, and prune so that the fungus will not bear fruit, for the ants feed on the sap of its roots, and sap is not formed after the plants bear fruit. When the queen leaves to start a new colony, she carries with her a tiny pill of fungus paste to start the next farm.

Army ants march through the jungles of Africa, South America, and Mexico in huge food searches. When they come to a river, groups of them form themselves into compact balls, roll into the river, and ride with the current to the other side. There they disembark from each other and continue their march. These ants have been in existence for thousands of years. Nature has preserved their remains beautifully intact in amber for all that time. The army ants that live today are exactly like those preserved in amber.

All these intricate and apparently intelligent things that various ants do would seem to indicate that they are creatures of high intelligence. Scientific experiments, however, have proved that ants act by instinct rather than by intelligence, and their intelligence is actually almost nonexistent. An ant's actions have therefore been preordained by an outside intelligence, just as the electronic brain was invented by man and comes up with good answers.

No one would ever think that such a machine came into existence gradually by itself. No one, then, can consistently believe that the tiny ants can do all the remarkable things they do without having had a Creator! This Creator is infinitely greater than any human inventor, for no machine has ever been invented that is as small as an ant and yet can perform so many complicated tasks!

MOTHS AND BUTTERFLIES

The beautiful butterfly flits to a certain bush. She is not interested at all in eating this bush, but here is where she lays her eggs, lustrous as pearls. This particular bush provides the perfect food for her particular offspring. How does she know? It is not intelligence, for even a human mother would not know that one certain bush in all the world was just the right food for her baby. No, it is God-given instinct.

The eggs hatch and become fuzzy earthbound caterpillars. They are somewhat repulsive to most of us. These caterpillars are like man born in sin; he is earthbound and spiritually ugly! The caterpillar builds a house of silk for himself. It is perfect on the first try! Here is the chrysalis he is tightly bound in for the winter. It is like man bound in sin. But wait! What is happening in this chrysalis as time passes? Jaws, claws, claspers, digestive system, and shape all begin to change! Head, legs, thorax, and wings begin to form! Some wonderful changes are taking place due to something greater than the caterpillar!

A corrosive liquid is voided which dissolves the silken chrysalis. Out of the broken container crawls a new creature, with wings crumpled and damp. It detects the redolent spring air and shakes itself. Its wings begin to spread out in the sunlight with exquisite grace. Their iridescent colors and jewellike tones flash as the butterfly lifts them in the air and flies heavenward.

This is a wonderful picture of what happens when a person is saved through Jesus Christ! While still in the chrysalis of sin (the flesh) a person cries out to the Lord to save him because of Christ's atonement. God reaches down and works a complete transformation in him. He is made a new creature (2 Co 5:17). Even while he is in that chrysalis he is a new creature, but it remains for the chrysalis to be broken before he emerges into the fulness of his new inheritance. So then when we leave this old body of our flesh, someday we shall be clothed with our new resurrection bodies, glorious as Christ's, without spot or blemish!

Bees

Bees are fascinating little creatures, just as complex in their way as the ants, and like them in many respects. When they organize a city, they build some 10,000 cells for honey and 12,000 cells for the larvae, a veritable citadel for the new queen. Producing wax from their own bodies, the bees build their cones in perfect symmetry and in the hexagonal shape that allows the maximum amount of double usage of walls. Further, their architectural structures are as fine as those of some great human architect! Can you imagine the knowledge that the master Architect of the universe must have instilled in each tiny bee brain in order for them to build like this?

There is excellent organization among the bees. Some are honey-collectors, some are nurses, some are fathers, and one only in each hive is the queen mother. She occupies herself solely with laying eggs. When the temperature around the hive gets too high, the bees organize into squads and set up a ventilating system with their fanning wings that would put an electric fan to shame! They thus maintain the exact temperature needed for the larvae.

While only one bee in every hive is the queen, there are many nurses who carefully tend the young. By the way in which they feed these young, they purposefully decide which ones will become queen bees and which workers. Although there may be hundreds of bees in a hive, no stranger bee is tolerated on the premises. The bees can tell by its odor if it does not belong!

Bees have a keen sense of direction. They fly and give each other directions by the sun. When one bee finds a source of honey it flies back to the hive and performs a symbolic little dance that not only tells the other bees exactly in which direction the honey is, but also exactly how far! The wings of bees are built like those on ship-borne aircraft. They are built in sections that fit together, for much the same reason that such aircraft are made like that. When they want to enter the hive, they just neatly fold up their double wings and crawl in. When they want to fly out they spread their wings, and the wings hook together for an effective spread.

Bees know all about wax-making, cell construction, royal jelly, the way to predetermine sex, nectar-gathering, and honey-making. They knew these things at the very beginning of their existence because these things are essential to their way of life. With them, as with the ants, it is not real intelligence, but a built-in, God-given instinct.

The supreme task of the bee, however, is its all-important function as chief plant pollinator. As it flits from flower to flower (always keeping to one particular kind at the time), it carries pollen with it on its fuzzy face. The flowers themselves are especially built for the bee's particular help. As the bee seeks to reach the nectar at the bottom, it needs to push the petals apart. As it does so, the pistil springs up and its stigma brushes the pollen off the bee's face that was picked up from the previous flower. The shorter stamens pop up with their fresh load of pollen and dust its face with a new load. Then the bee flies to the next flower to get more honey and continues the great task the Lord created it to do.

God's Little Undertakers

The sexton beetle and his mate are probably the most industrious and useful of beetles in existence. Just as the bees, they too have a God-given task, an important one. They are the dead body cleanup crew. Working together, male and female take all night to carry a dead body of some creature to soft ground to bury it. The little male beetle gets under the body (perhaps a rabbit) and prepares to heave it. The female clears the ground ahead of impeding twigs and stones. The male pushes, the female pulls.

Before they start this process, however, the sexton (being a good undertaker) makes sure the animal is really dead. He makes a complete and thorough examination of the body. Only when he is satisfied it is really a corpse, does he begin his work.

When they finally get the body to the burial spot, they begin to work under it, removing dirt. Slowly the body descends into its last resting place. Now the beetles pluck off its fur in full preparation for its destiny. Then they make a little chamber nearby, and there the female lays her eggs. While waiting for the eggs to hatch and grubs to grow, they live in their snug little apartment, well supplied with handy meat.

Isn't this a great amount of knowledge for one little beetle to have? Isn't it interesting that all of his particular kind have this wisdom? Who taught these little fellows all these things in the first place? How does each sexton beetle offspring know what to do without being taught? The sexton beetle is just another example of God's hand in creation, of God-given instinct.

Interesting Insect Information

An insect has an entirely different way of breathing than that of any animal. It does not have a pumping type of respiration. Air merely comes into its body through a number of apertures in its trunk. This is one of the main reasons why an insect never grows very big, because no part of its body can be too far from the nearest air intake. There is such a tremendous difference between the respiratory systems of insects, fish, and beasts that one wonders what explanation can logically be given by those who believe that everything simply evolved.

The moss agate is said to have been formed when the earth was young. Yet, a mosquito has been found entombed in a moss agate. It is much like our famous New Jersey mosquitoes today. The female mosquito is especially built to drill through skin in order to get her meals of blood. She has six neat tools built into her lower lip: a pair of lancets, a pair of saws, a syringe, and a syphon. She is at least as ingenious an invention as a doctor's set of surgical instruments.

A termite lives on a diet of wood, but he is not able to digest that wood. So God conveniently supplied the termite with a host of animalcules (tiny one-celled animals), as well as bacteria, to digest it for him and turn it into real nourishment after he sends it down to his stomach.

A grasshopper can leap twenty times its own length. A dragonfly has compound eyes that occupy most of his head, and he has 25,000 views to see. A tiny midge has wings that beat 2,000 times a second. Flies and butterflies are able to detect the tiniest bit of sweetness. While man can taste one part of sugar in 200, a fly can detect one part in 40,000, and a butterfly can detect one part in 300,000! These are all special wonders that can help us to see the hand of a great Creator even in the little world of insects.

SPIDERS (ARACHNIDS)

Spiders have been saved until last because, rightly speaking, they are not insects, although we tend to think of them in that general category. There are, however, 30,000 species of *arachnida*, so they compose a large portion of creatures by themselves. Numbered with the spiders in this group are scorpions, mites, and ticks.

Spiders can spin seven different kinds of silk, and one individual spider can spin five different kinds. Each species, however, spins its own particular kind of web just as its ancestors did. Usually the web is spun like a wheel spoke with about twenty-one spokes stretching out from the center. The spider then circles these with supporting strands of silk. Over this initial dry web the spider runs a gummy sticky thread which she herself fastidiously avoids after spinning, for it is only for the prey. This orb web of the spider is a marvelous engineering job and would do credit to the best-trained engineer. Its circles and spokes are geometrically accurate, yet there are thousands of separate parts.

Trapdoor spiders build tunnels for their homes and fit them with hinged trapdoors. Water spiders make watertight air chambers under water and transport bubbles of air into it until their families are raised. They also make rafts to sail on the surface of the water. Balloon spiders spin parachutes of silk and then travel sometimes many miles through the air on them.

Spiders have been found nearly three miles above the earth's surface.

These spiders are surely the work of God too, for no little creatures such as they could possibly have the brains or even the instinct to spin such geometrical masterpieces without a master Engineer as their Maker!

THE JUDGMENTS OF GOD

> He spake, and there came divers sorts of flies, and lice in all their coasts. He spake, and the locusts came, and caterpillers, and that without number, and did eat up all the herbs in their land, and devoured the fruit of their ground (Ps 105:31, 34-35).

Many people today seem to have the impression that if there is a God, He is an easygoing God of love. It is true that the great love of God for mankind was revealed beautifully in and through the Lord Jesus Christ, His Son. However, Jesus also revealed His Father as a holy God who could not countenance sin and rebellion. Even the loving but holy Jesus said, "The Son of Man shall send forth his angels, and they shall gather out of his kingdom all things that offend, and them which do iniquity; and shall cast them into a furnace of fire: there shall be wailing and gnashing of teeth" (Mt 13:41-42).

Some of the greatest judgments God brought upon man here on earth occurred when Pharaoh would not let God's people Israel go out of Egypt. There were ten horrible judgments in all, and in some of these God used insects of various kinds.

God covered the land and people with lice. Pharaoh

had promised to let the Israelites go, but after the plague was lifted he backed down. Then God filled the land with great swarms of flies. Later locusts and caterpillars were sent to devour the crops. Thus it is seen that some of these insects with great nuisance value were actually used by God not only for judgment, but also, in this case, for the welfare of His chosen people. His chosen people, Israel, were completely bypassed by all these terrible plagues.

The Bible predicts that in the last days, among other judgments of God on godless men, will be something called "locusts." "And in those days shall men seek death, and shall not find it; and shall desire to die, and death shall flee from them" (Rev 9:6).

How can this awful time of judgment be avoided? Many of the prophecies in the Bible pertaining to the end time have already come true. Israel has once again become a nation. The Common Market in Europe seems to be heading toward a United States of Europe, a revival of the old Roman Empire perhaps. The churches all talk about uniting. There is a great ecumenical movement afoot. This could give rise to the super church of the end times that gives worship to the antichrist. People run to and fro more than ever. There have been earthquakes and wars and rumors of wars in recent times more than ever before in history! Jesus said, "So likewise ye, when ye shall see all these things, know that it is near, even at the doors" (Mt 24:33).

Just before these judgments come on the earth something wonderful is going to happen!

> For as in the days that were before the flood they were eating and drinking, marrying and giving in marriage, until the day that Noe entered into the ark, and knew not until the flood came, and took them all away; so shall also the coming of the Son of man be. Then shall two be in the field; the one shall be taken, and the other left. Two women shall be grinding at the mill; the one shall be taken, and the other left. Watch therefore: for ye know not what hour your Lord doth come (Mt 24:38-42).

Just before the rains came, God led Noah and his family safely into the ark. The ark is symbolic of Jesus Christ. Those who are "in Him" (that is, trust in Him for their salvation) are safe from all of God's great general judgments on mankind. Just before God brings the great judgments of Revelation to pass, all the true Christians will be caught up into the clouds to be with Christ (1 Th 4:14-18). "For God hath not appointed us to wrath, but to obtain salvation by our Lord Jesus Christ" (1 Th 5:9).

All then who would be saved from the judgments of God—not only on mankind but also on all lost sinners—need to cry out to God: "God, be merciful to me a sinner, and save me for Jesus' sake!" This is the cry God answers for anyone, for God is "not willing that any should perish" (2 Pe 3:9).

"Believe on the Lord Jesus Christ, and thou shalt be saved" (Ac 16:31).

7

SEA CREATURES

> O LORD, how manifold are thy works! In wisdom hast thou made them all: the earth is full of thy riches. So is this great and wide sea, wherein are things creeping innumerable, both small and great beasts (Ps 104:24-25).

WHAT IS THIS STRANGE, porpoiselike thing gliding through the water? It is huge, like a whale. As we approach it, we discover it is not a sea creature; it is a man-made thing, a submarine.

Made of steel, it is a wonderful invention built to withstand the pressures of water and depth. Within are men who must have oxygen to breathe and live. But this need has been foreseen, for there is adequate oxygen within the watertight hull, as well as adequate lighting. Careful preparation has been made for the great depths to which this marvel descends.

Many and varied instruments guide this vessel's way through the murky depths. Well-trained men read these instruments, not only to keep the ship precisely on course toward its destination, but also to discover if there are any other vessels nearby.

Another craft approaches on the surface of the sea. It drops anchor, and a man leans over the railing and looks at the glistening water. On his feet are two strange slippers which resemble fins. On his face is a mask, and on his back two tanks of oxygen. He adjusts his face mask carefully, then plunges into the icy waters. Slowly he presses his way downward. After gathering the specimens he is seeking, he takes great care to come up even slower than he descended so that he will not be a victim of what is called "the bends."

Miles away his brother descends in another type of suit, one much heavier and topped with a cumbersome dome for his head. His air is pumped through a tube from the ship above him. His suit allows him to descend to even greater depths than his brother. A diving bell is also used by this ship to survey the deep waters below with its great searching beams.

Truly man has conquered great depths of the oceans, as well as the heights of the sky, through his amazing inventions. But God was before him in this also, for He made creatures uniquely fitted for living in the sea, and their equipment has been duplicated to a large extent by sea-exploring men. Most bony fish, for instance, have air bladders that enable them to float at various depths, according to the amount of oxygen present. Creatures of great fragility, such as the jellyfish and glass sponge, live under immense pressure in the deep sea. God has equipped them with special pressure in their tissues to live in their special environment.

A number of deep-sea fish have "headlights," and the great Gulper Eel, which is fifty-five inches long, has a red "taillight." Indeed, some fish look much like railroad trains, with rows of lights along their sides. Other fish carry luminous torches that can be turned on or off at will. Still others are illuminated all over, like a cruise steamer filled with happy vacationers.

Although whales and seals are warm-blooded mammals like ourselves, they are able to dive straight down to a depth of half a mile and yet return immediately to the surface. Such a dive would probably kill a human being, who develops caisson disease if brought up too rapidly from just 200 feet of water. Even more amazing are the tiny shrimps and other planktonic creatures that move up and down thousands of feet in the water, constantly adjusting to each new amount of pressure with apparently no trouble. And long before man had jet planes and atomic-powered submarines, God's jet-propelled rocket, the squid, made his way through the oceanic currents.

The Bible says that God made each creature "after his kind." When we consider there are 14,000 species of fish, 80,000 species of mollusks or shellfish, 5,000 species of corals and their kin, 3,000 species of sponges, and 2,500 species of crustacea (crabs, lobster, shrimp, etc.), each species perfectly adapted to its particular environment and way of life, then we begin to perceive the enormity and intricacy of God's creation! Evolution does not adequately account for the perfection of adaptation that we find in all of God's sea creatures. Only a special and particular creation can.

Propagation

A further fact of interest is that each creature breeds with its own kind. A flounder mates with a flounder, a tuna with a tuna, a crawfish with a crawfish, and so on. And these many variations of sea life have almost as many variations in propagating "their kind." In general most female fish lay the eggs, and the male fish fertilizes them. But the variations lay in how each species goes about this process and the care of their eggs. For instance, the Tipalia female lays her eggs, then the male catches them in his mouth and carries them there for eleven days, until and after they hatch. While certain other fish will eat their offspring, this father fish goes without food for these eleven days in order to give his babies a good start in life.

Grunions at spawning time permit themselves to be washed ashore with high tides just before the tide goes out (as any Californian grunion-catcher can attest). The female lays her eggs, the male fertilizes them; then they flop their way back to the ocean, leaving their eggs to incubate in the warm sand. Two weeks later, when the tide comes in again, the eggs hatch explosively and the newborn grunions swim matter-of-factly out into the ocean.

The salmon of the Pacific Ocean are born in quiet headwaters of rivers and streams that run through the far northwest corner of the United States and empty into the Pacific. When sufficiently grown, they follow these rivers toward the ocean, where they "go out into the great big world" for several years. When the proper time comes, instinct calls them back to the little stream where they were born; they make their way across the trackless Pacific to the very river out of which they came several years before. Fighting the current, they proceed to their very birthplace, where they bring into existence the coming generation.

Eels from European waters go through much the same process. They journey 3,000 miles to the Sargasso Sea to spawn. Their larvae, when large enough, make the long journey back to the place their parents had been, taking several years to make the trip. They find their way unerringly through the vast sea.

Are not these feats amazing? Could such perfection in direction-finding have evolved any more than our own compass has? Yet we read these wonderful words in God's book: "What is man, that thou art mindful of him? Thou madest him to have dominion over the works of thy hands ... the fish of the sea, and whatsoever passeth through the paths of the seas" (Ps 8:4, 6-8).

Physical Wonders

Sea life varies greatly in size. Tiny, microscopic creatures are part of the plankton world; some are as delicate and lacy as snowflakes. The plankton among which they live is composed of an enormous variety of small and perfect sea creatures and plants. This plankton provides many larger sea creatures with food. In contrast to these tiny creations are enormous whales, sharks, and fish that inhabit the deeps. Some of these huge creatures weigh many tons. Can one imagine how much food they must consume in order to live? Yet the Bible says, "There is that leviathan, whom thou hast made to play therein. These wait all upon thee; that thou mayest give them their meat in due season" (Ps 104:26-27).

All of these creatures, great and small, are better chemists in one respect than men, for they are able to find and use the mineral wealth of the sea to a much greater degree of success. Many of them utilize the cobalt, nickel, copper, vanadium, and other minerals for their bodily welfare and existence. Through a large number of good-tasting sea dwellers God makes these rich resources of the sea available to man in the form of food. Some nations of people exist almost entirely on food from God's watery storehouse.

Consider some of the physical wonders in sea creatures. The deep-sea angler, for instance, catches other fish like a fisherman; he uses lures, lines, and hooks. Yet he never patronizes a sports store; he got all his equipment straight from God. The horseshoe crab can detect the position of the sun and moves by it, even if he cannot see it. Horseshoe crabs have used the polarity of the sun for thousands of years to guide their movements; man has just become aware of it in the last half century.

Crabs can grow new claws, lobsters can grow new eyes, and fish can grow new teeth whenever these creatures happen to lose them. They actually have a faculty which man does not enjoy.

The oyster defies many elementary rules of biology. He has neither head nor tail, and no detectable brain.

He has a remarkable pumping and filtering system however. The oyster feeds only when the quality of the water meets certain requirements, that is, when it is not polluted. He makes his own home in a definite shape; he manufactures his shell through an intricate process. By starting with an irritant (usually a grain of sand) he manufactures a pearl, a beautiful jewel that never requires polishing or cutting to improve its natural beauty. Here we find a startling combination of waterworks, housebuilder, and jewel producer in an apparently brainless creature!

The flounder starts life as an ordinary round fish. As it grows, it flattens out and its left eye moves toward the right until both eyes are on the top side of the now flat fish, its white underpart lying on the bottom of the sea. In several other species of fish that go through a similar process of development, it is the right eye that changes place. But always the same eye in the same species is the one that moves! These fish, as well as many others, can also change color to blend with their surroundings.

Eyes and Ears

Although most sea creatures do not have eyes with true lenses, the octopus, squid, and cattlefish do; and they have most specialized eyes. Crayfish and lobster have compound eyes on stalks that can be moved around for better vision. The fish that would most interest the optician, optometrist, and middle-aged people, however, is the one with "bifocal eyes" that lives in the rivers and estuaries of the Caribbean. Since his food floats on the top of the water, one set of pupils is to see in the air above the water; a second set watches where he is going through the water.

Fish have ears entirely different from land dwellers. They have "ear stones" in two chambers in their skull that enable them to hear and maintain balance. These creatures had to have these organs from the very beginning of their existence or they could not have been fish, any more than a telephone could do its work without a receiver.

Color

Just as with birds and animals, God has given the camouflage of coloring to fish. Fish who live near the shore are mottled and striped to blend in with their surroundings. Surface fish are blue, or mottled blue and green. Those that inhabit the deeper, darker waters may be a brilliant blue, and many creatures at the intermediate level between surface and bottom are crystal clear. At depths greater than 1,500 feet, all the fish are black, brown violet, or red. Fish tend to blend with the color of the sea at their particular strata.

The wrasse can change its brilliant colors to that of any fish with which it comes into contact. On the other hand, the moonfish comes in unchangeable rainbow colors and the Siamese fighting fish in gorgeous red, blue, green, lavender, and orchid varieties. In addition to coloring fish for their protection, God has seen to it that some are enabled by their environment to uphold His gift of beautiful things to the world of men. Below the glistening surface of the sea abide some of the most beautiful creatures in all the world. Tinted with iridescent jewellike hues, they weave their graceful way through the undersea gardens, symmetrical and often luminous.

Protection, Offense, and Defense

Besides being protected by their coloring, sea creatures have other means of protection and of offense and defense. The file fish feeds among clumps of eelgrass. In times of danger he stands on his nose, his fins gently waving to imitate a clump of grass; he matches perfectly! The globefish swells himself with air and rides the current to safety. The porcupine fish similarly swells. Since he is ball-like and prickly, other fish leave him alone. The climbing perce of Burma climbs trees. When he seeks safety in another pool and gets thirsty enroute, he climbs a tree to get at water in the hollow of the tree.

The squid ejects a cloud of ink to escape his enemies, and the deep-sea squid ejects a luminous cloud in the depths because that does a better job of hiding him. The swordfish, a beautifully streamlined, fifteen-foot danger, has a sword so powerful it has been known to penetrate several inches of solid oak; it is stronger than the strongest sword.

Some crabs carry poisonous sea anemones for protection. The Dromia crab carries an offensive sponge on its back for camouflage and safety. The spider crab cuts seaweed and deliberately attaches it to its back, where the seaweed starts to grow. If the crab is transplanted to a different location, he will divest himself of the seaweed and plant local camouflage.

The electric eel that lives in the backwaters of the Amazon sends out discharges up to 500 volts many times each minute. Thus he charges the water at the approach of an enemy. The electric catfish uses his "stunning" charge to give other fish a shock and steal their food. The electric ray has a very complicated setup of electric parts, with 450 tubes in each organ to supply positive and negative currents. He has many electric plates and also "batteries." His charge is so strong it can knock a man flat on the ground.

Certainly we are rightly proud of the electrical devices and systems we have been able to develop in recent years. What a boon are the electric light, electric heating, appliances of all sorts, radio, television, batteries, and so many other things we take for granted! But God installed these principles in some of His sea creatures thousands of years ago, and their offspring are still born with them. We can no more say they evolved to this than we could say that these marvelous inventions of man came hodge-podge into being after enough lightning had struck the earth!

Fossils and Their Ancestors

Sea creatures and their fossils prove rather embarrassing to the evolutionist. Shellfish, sharks, limpets, oysters, turtles, whelks, coral, crabs, and fish are the same today as their ancestors have been for centuries. Recently a frill shark, similar to the most ancient shark fossils, was captured off Santa Barbara, California. Others of his species have been caught in Japanese and Norwegian waters.

A very interesting fish was caught alive in the trawl in December, 1938, off the southeast tip of Africa. It was a bright blue fish that was *supposed* to have been extinct for at least 60 million years. Imagine, a fish which supposedly had had 60 million years in which to evolve, yet he was still the same! The answer is: he is still the same as God, his Creator, made him.

Thousands of years ago crayfish were abundant, and they are still in existence today in the same form that they were then. They are among the oldest living orders today. In the Pacific Coast range fossils of the so-called Eocene period are found in tremendous profusion. Gigantic sharks and immense whales are imbedded seven or eight thousand feet above the sea, forty miles from the nearest beach. They appear to be very much like their present-day descendants.

Coral is the body of a small insect. By the process of living and dying, these minute creatures have succeeded in building up islands. Although these polyps have been industriously working for thousands of years, their descendants in existence today appear to be identical to the original coral polyps. It is claimed these polyps have been in existence for millions of years, yet there has been no apparent change whatsoever in this animal.

After all this evidence, we must conclude that each kind of creature in the sea must have been the result of a particular act of creation by God.

Fish, Nets, and Jonah

In the days of Jesus Christ the commonest types of food eaten were fish and bread. When Christ fed 5,000 men, plus women and children, He did it by breaking up two small fishes and five loaves that a little boy had brought for lunch. Although it has been claimed in recent years by highly educated men that this was an impossibility, still it was surely no more an impossibility for God in the flesh to do than it has been for men to split the tiny atom and create the most devastating explosion the world has ever known. Science knows now that in every atom there is vastly more space than there is matter. God always knew that.

Jesus compared the kingdom of heaven to "a net, that was cast into the sea, and gathered of every kind." "Which, when it was full," He said, "they drew to shore, and sat down, and gathered the good into vessels, but cast the bad away. So shall it be at the end of the world: the angels shall come forth, and sever the wicked from among the just, and shall cast them into the furnace of fire: there shall be wailing and gnashing of teeth" (Mt 13:48-50).

Although multitudes of people all over the world are members of professing Christendom, they are like the fish in that net, to be sorted out according to good and bad. Since the only way any human being can become "good" in God's sight is by being washed of his sins by the shed blood of Jesus Christ, all those who have not been thus cleansed will be adjudged "bad" and cast into the lake of fire. However, as long as a person is alive, he has the opportunity to cry out to God as the publican did: "God, be merciful to me, a sinner!"

At least four, and perhaps more, of Jesus' disciples were fishermen. Jesus called them into His service in a unique fashion. Peter, Andrew, James, and John had been fishing all night and had taken in nothing. Jesus told them, "Launch out into the deep, and let down your nets for a draught." Although they hardly expected to catch anything, they did as they were told, and caught so many fish it almost broke their nets.

Peter fell down before Jesus and cried, "Depart from me, for I am a sinful man, O Lord!"

And Jesus said to him, "Fear not; from henceforth thou shalt catch men. Follow me, and I will make you fishers of men." And they straightway left their nets, and followed Him.

This is the same sort of reaction Jesus Christ desires of His disciples today. He wants us "to launch out into the deep" in faith, not to cling to the shoreline of always safe and lukewarm discipleship. He wants us to fully trust Him and His leadership and guidance. He wants to use our lips, our minds, and our talents to win others to Him. He wants us to cast out the net of the Gospel so that His Spirit can fill it with the precious souls of men.

One of Jesus' most profound prophecies referred to a sea creature. To the Pharisees who asked for a sign, Jesus said, "An evil and adulterous generation seeketh after a sign; and there shall no sign be given to it, but the sign of the prophet Jonas. For as Jonas was three days and three nights in the whale's belly, so shall the Son of Man be three days and three nights in the heart of the earth" (Mt 12:39-40). Jesus was prophesying here not only His coming death, but also His resurrection after three days. Jesus was also giving full authentication to the story of Jonah and the great fish (popularly referred to as a whale).

There are many people who scoff at the story of Jonah, and because of that story they will not believe the rest of the Bible. Many of them claim to be followers of Jesus Christ and His teachings. But if a person scoffs at the story of Jonah and the great fish, how can he sensibly follow the teachings of a man who believed not only that story but the whole Old Testament?

Actually it has been discovered that some whales and fish have large chambers filled with air in their heads. When they take into their mouths anything too large to be comfortably swallowed, this object is impelled into this chamber in their heads. Both a man and a dog have been known to survive this strange experience. So it was scientifically possible for Jonah to have been swallowed by a whale or large fish and come out alive. At any rate, the Bible says, "The LORD had prepared a great fish to swallow up Jonah" (Jon 1:17). Certainly if God made this marvelous universe of ours, it was but a small thing for Him to do!

The story of Jonah and the great fish is a wonderful story of God's compassion on a wicked nation and of His sending a messenger to them to tell them to repent. The primary meaning of it, however, lies in its symbolic prophecy concerning what would happen to Jesus, the Son of God. Jesus was put to death as He prophesied, but He rose again from the grave after three days, also as He prophesied. We serve a living Saviour today, One who says to us, "Follow me; I will make you fishers of men."

8

REPTILES AND AMPHIBIANS

> And God made the beast of the earth after his
> kind, and cattle after their kind, and every thing
> that creepeth upon the earth after his kind: and
> God saw that it was good (Gen 1:25).

THE BEAUTIFULLY COLORED SHINING ONE moved slowly toward the unsuspecting young woman as she lay languidly in the fragrant bower. As he approached her, she glanced up and thought, "Oh, there's the one that Adam called 'Serpent.' He certainly is a pretty thing!"

Serpent halted in front of the woman. "Hello, Eve," he said in a friendly tone. "How are things with you today?"

"Oh, I'm feeling all right," she answered, "but I am quite lonesome today. Adam had to go take care of the far side of the garden, and I don't know when he'll be home."

"It seems a shame that God has only created two humans, you and Adam," Serpent consoled.

Eve put up her hand in protest. "Oh, I'm not complaining!" she answered quickly. "God has been very good to us. He has given us this beautiful garden in which to live, and He comes to visit and talk with us every evening." She reached up and plucked a grape from a bunch hanging nearby and slipped the juicy morsel into her mouth. "And God has given us all these delicious things here to eat."

"Yea," said Serpent in a left-hand agreement, "but has God not said, 'You shall not eat of every tree of the garden'?"

Eve looked at him puzzled. Now why did he have to bring that up? "We may eat of the fruit of the trees of the garden," she said slowly, "but of the fruit of the tree which is here in the middle of the garden God has said, 'You shall not eat of it, neither shall you touch it—" Eve paused, her voice wavered, "lest you die."

"Oh, come now, Eve," Serpent commented jovially, "you shall not surely die! You see, the reason God doesn't want you and Adam to eat of that tree is because He knows that the day you do so your eyes will be opened, and you will be as gods, knowing good and evil!"

After Eve thought about it for a while, her heart was in a turmoil. What if it were true that God was in reality trying to keep Adam and her from realizing their full potentiality? She strolled to the clearing where the tree of the knowledge of good and evil was located, and sat contemplating it for a while.

The longer she looked at it, the more tempting the fruit seemed to become. It was luscious and toothsome, that was plain to see. Eve came to her decision.

She arose, went over to the tree, reached up and plucked the delectable-looking fruit. Her teeth sank into its delightful flesh, and she tasted it to the full.

Eve suddenly cried out! What had happened to her? She felt strange. She looked down at herself and instantly wanted to cover herself with some of the nearby fig leaves. A pang of guilt struck her heart. What had she done?

Suddenly she saw Adam come walking into the clearing. She called out to him, trying to sound cheerful. "Adam, oh Adam, come over here!"

"Eve, what are you doing with that fruit in your hand?" Adam exclaimed in horror.

Eve sidled over by Adam and put her arm affectionately through his, raising the fruit to his lips. "Adam, we've been misled. See, I have eaten the fruit and I am not dead. In fact, I suddenly seem to have wisdom that I never had before! Here, taste this, it's by far the most delicious fruit in the garden!"

Thus Adam also ate of the forbidden fruit, and the bondage and penalty of sin fell on all the human race through him, their ancestor. Some people try to mythologize or laugh off this account, but they cannot deny the ravages of sin that we see all about us today, as well as down through history. Disease, crime, tragedy, famine, and death were in the forbidden fruit that Adam and Eve partook of on that fatal day. These have stalked Adam's descendants down through the centuries. But the worst thing that came from Adam and Eve's disobedience to God was the separation of mankind from God because of sin entering in.

Did all this come about through an unintelligent

serpent, a beast of the field? No, indeed, for just as the first book of the Bible presents Satan as being a mastermind of craftiness, so the last book in the Bible says, "And the great dragon was cast out, that old serpent, called the Devil, and Satan, which deceiveth the whole world" (Rev 12:9). The serpent was the instrument used by Satan to corrupt the human race, for it was also a subtle creature, and still is to this day. Snakes are known for their deadly cunning and their remarkable ability to strike quickly, thus a snake is an excellent symbol and representative for Satan.

But God Made the Snakes

In spite of one of their species having been used by the fallen archangel, Satan, for his nefarious purpose, snakes are still creations of God; they show His handiwork in their physiques and instincts.

The head of a snake is plated with scales. Snakes are cold-blooded creatures but do not have gills. They are deaf, for they have no ears, but they "hear" by feeling ground vibrations. They have no eyelids, but their eyes are permanently covered with a protective transparent membrane.

A snake can unhinge its upper and lower jaws and work them independently. Because of this, it can hold and pull in a large prey between these jaws. Since its skin, ribs, and organs are highly flexible, it can engulf a prey perhaps three times its own diameter. Snakes swallow their prey whole, and their powerful digestive juices do the rest. It is remarkable that when the Lord does not think it practical to provide a creature with teeth to chew, He does provide it with a flexible physique and the proper digestive juices.

Another remarkable thing in connection with snakes and teeth is that in the case of snakes hatched from eggs, the babies are equipped with a special "egg tooth" with which they rip their way out of their eggs. After a week or two this handy one-job tool disappears.

Poisonous Snakes

God also has provided certain snakes with poisonous venom and, contrary to the beliefs of some that mankind is "target for the day," this poisonous venom was given to the snakes to help them get their dinners. Actually snakes try to stay clear of man as much as possible. They are mainly interested in finding some juicy morsel or sunny ledge or dark, comfortable burrow.

Pit vipers (copperheads, water moccasins, rattlesnakes) are equipped with two long, hollow teeth. When the snake's mouth flies open, these fangs spring into position. A sheath of thin translucent flesh is withdrawn from the fangs when the reptile strikes. Venom contained in a pair of salivary glands near the eyes goes through the fangs into the wound. Every month the viper gets a new set of fangs. Truly the fangs of a pit viper are as great a marvel as a hypodermic needle, and needed an inventor just as much. The pit vipers have pits on their faces with which they can sense temperature variations in their vicinity and can thus detect the presence of warm-blooded prey. They had thermometers long before man invented them.

Coral snakes, cobras, and mambas have a different arrangement for their fangs. They have short fangs which are rigidly set in the upper jaw and permanently erect. Instead of breaking down the red blood cells, as the venom of the pit viper does, their venom attacks and paralyzes the nerve centers. Although this poison is very potent and dangerous, the even temper of the snake makes it quite unlikely that a person would be bitten by these snakes. Again, their main interest is in getting a good meal, and that is why God gave them these poisonous fangs.

Some may wonder why God made such predatory creatures as snakes. In God's balance of nature, snakes keep down the population of rats and other such mammals that might overrun the world but for their natural enemies.

Snakes: A Boon to Mankind

What a snake considers a good meal usually consists of that which man considers a terrible scourge or pest. Rats, mice, gophers, chipmunks, moles, squirrels, as well as harmful insects, are juicy morsels as far as a snake is concerned. In the wheat belt, the bull snake keeps down the rodent population. The gopher snake, the yellow rat snake, the fox snake, the milk snake, as well as others of their clan, do the farmers an inestimable service. Since the depredations of rodents on crops run into millions of dollars, who knows what would be left if our snake friends did not have their particular dietary tastes? Perhaps if such war were not waged by man on the snake population, the depredations that are done now by the rodents would not be nearly what they are. God has provided balance in nature. Whenever man disturbs that balance, he suffers from it.

BEAUTY OF SNAKES

Many snakes are extraordinarily beautiful, coming in every gorgeous color from flaming crimson to bluish green. None of them come in just one color, but are striped or banded or spotted with various colors. The rainbow snake, for instance, has three longitudinal stripes of dark red or rich orange on a purplish black or deep blue background. On each side of these stripes runs one band of pale yellow. The snake's lower part is pinkish red with black blotches. On top of all this riot of color, it has a glassy polished appearance. Thus God has even lavished beauty and color on His lowly creation, the snake.

THE HOUSE CARRIERS: TURTLES

Turtles are the only vertebrates that carry their own house with them. These houses are sturdy, interestingly marked shells. A turtle can pull its head and feet within the shell for protection. The box turtle can even completely seal himself in. Turtles have no teeth, but the Lord has equipped them with beaklike jaws.

Most turtles are good swimmers. They can also float on the water. Sea turtles have flippers instead of legs because they live in the water and not on land as do their cousins. Within "kinds," defined by Webster as "a natural group, class, or division," there can be a lot of variation so that each species is best adapted to its environment. This in no way indicates, however, that the great gap between kinds can be, or ever has been, bridged.

Turtles do the job for God and man of being scavengers, as well as eating harmful insects and their larvae. They are also a good source of food for man.

CROCODILIA

Crocodiles, alligators, and gavials are just as beautifully armor-plated as a tank, and their heads are nearly solid bone. Their long, powerful tails serve as fine weapons, and they are also equipped with powerful jaws containing sharp conical teeth. The Lord has provided crocodiles with an unusual teeth-cleaning plan: little ploverlike birds, which hop fearlessly in and out of their mouths, prune their teeth for toothsome leftovers!

THE VERSATILE LIZARDS

Here one flies through the air from one tree to another like a flying squirrel. There we see another one swimming through the water as expertly as a crocodile. A third one runs through the rocks so swiftly that our eyes can hardly follow him. A fourth one sits on a rock sunning himself; and if we had not observed his ascent to the rock, we probably would not notice him there, for he is the same color as the rock. These are the versatile lizards.

Unlike the snakes, lizards have nonexpansible mouths, but God has provided them with teeth which snakes do not have. Also unlike snakes, lizards have movable eyelids and external ear openings. Since their bodies do not glide on the ground the way snakes' bodies do, they cannot "hear" through their bodies, and so the Lord gave them ears. Perhaps the most unusual gift that lizards have is the ability to grow new tails. Since the part of them most likely to be caught first by an enemy is their tail, the advantage they have in being able to quickly shed this tail and leave it behind with the enemy can readily be seen. Before long they have grown a brand-new tail, and they can also grow new teeth to replace old ones.

Lizards come in many beautiful colors and designs just as snakes do. The collared lizard, for instance, has a green upper surface covered with yellowish white dots, a coloring changeable at the creature's will. It has one white and two black rings around its neck, its throat is orange, and its lower surface pale blue white. And, of course, almost everyone is familiar with the chameleon, which can also change color at will. When frightened or engaged in fighting, he turns a brilliant green. When resting, he is a deep gray or brown. The brown-shouldered uta is colored to blend into whatever his surroundings are; in the desert the utas are one color, and in red sandstone areas they are another.

Salamanders and Newts

These little fellows can not only reproduce new tails when the old ones are lost, but they can also grow new limbs. In addition, they all have the ability to change their colors to match their backgrounds. These creatures, too, have beautiful and interesting markings.

The tiger salamander is another wonderful product of God's providential hand. Since instant and evolution are two words that are basically contradictory to one another, then we must see God's creation in this salamander. In the southwest United States and Mexico this amphibian never leaves the larval stage; he retains gills, stays in the water, and is perfectly able to breed. Should the water dry up, he is also perfectly capable of transforming into the adult land salamander!

The spotted newt is born in the water and spends the first few months there since he has gills. Then he develops lungs, emerges from the water, and becomes a land-dweller for several years. Then his dorsal ridge disappears, his tail becomes heavily finned like a tadpole tail, and he returns to the water. There is certainly no reasonable explanation for this type of development outside of the creative hand of God and His knowledge of what is best for this particular salamander.

TOADS AND FROGS: GILLS AND LUNGS

These little creatures are just as much a marvel of design and combination from a master Creator as the amazing invention called television, with its picture and sound, is the product of a number of intelligent inventors.

They begin life as underwater tadpoles with gills

and a long eellike tail. Then four legs miraculously appear; the tail disappears; lungs develop, replacing the gills; the mouth structure changes, and presto, we have a land-living toad or frog instead of a tadpole! This metamorphosis has been going on for thousands of years (there was a plague of frogs in Moses' day), but the toads and frogs have always started life as tadpoles and have always turned into air-breathing toads and frogs.

These fellows provide welcome signs of spring with their shrill trills. During a quiet summer night in the country one can hear their croaks blended in chorus with the sounds of crickets and locusts. It seems to find a place among the sweetest, most tranquilizing music ever heard. Toads and frogs are a great boon to mankind and best friends to the farmer, for they dispose of large quantities of flies, grubs, worms, slugs, beetles, and grasshoppers. (They are also considered good friends by small boys.)

TOADS

A toad's tongue is attached by its tip to the front of his lower jaw. When he opens his mouth, his tongue hurls out its entire length and catches a fly or insect on its sticky surface. Instantly it whips back into the toad's mouth with the juicy morsel. Toads have beautiful, jewellike eyes with velvety black oval pupils, surrounded by glittering golden irises that pop out like gems in a ring. They can puff out their bodies like balloons when annoyed or frightened. By inflating their huge neck sacs, some of them can make a chorus of shrill chirps, bleatings, croaks, or squawks.

The spadefoot toad has spadelike back feet to use for burrowing. When in danger he can dig backward and thus can rapidly melt into the ground. The horned toad, because he is rather slow, is colored to blend in with his surroundings, and he has a spiny crown that makes him a disagreeable creature to swallow. His habit of ejecting a thin stream of blood from his eyes when alarmed makes him even more unpopular with his potential enemies.

The midwife toad takes the eggs from his mate, loops them around his hind legs, scoops a hole in the mud for himself and the eggs, and waits for them to incubate. After a few weeks he jumps into the water, towing the string. The eggs are broken by the rush of water against them and the tadpoles swim out into their made-to-order environment.

Who gave the midwife toad the instinct to do all these things to help the propagation of his kind? What is it that makes an unintelligent creature like this sit for several weeks incubating eggs and probably going hungry? How does he know exactly the right time for the eggs to be pulled into the water so that the little tads will enjoy ideal birth conditions? The answer is, God made him so.

FROGS

Frogs have legs especially built for leaping. The two-inch wood frog, for instance, can leap four or five feet. Frogs, as well as salamanders, can change their colors to blend safely into their backgrounds. The tree frogs are especially adept at this. They turn leafy green when on a plant, brown on the ground, silvery gray tinged with green and darker gray markings when clinging to the trunk of a tree. Tree frogs have four fingers on front legs and five toes on back, complete with sucking pads, to uniquely equip them for tree climbing.

Bull frogs are also specially designed so that they are able to close their nostrils and absorb oxygen from water through their skin. Thus they can lie quietly at the bottom of their pond a large part of the time.

God's Judgment on Sin

Although reptiles and amphibians serve a useful purpose in God's economy here on earth, they are used symbolically in the Bible to depict sin or God's judgment on sin. It is significant that they are listed among the unclean creatures in the laws given to Moses; they were called an "abomination." Since sin is an abomination to God, it is not hard to see why this group of creatures is used symbolically in connection with sin.

The first entrance of sin into the human race came about through Satan, appearing in the guise of a serpent. Just as a lamb in the Scriptures is emblematic of our Lord Jesus Christ, so a serpent seems to be most symbolic of Satan. Almost invariably the serpent is preeminent in cults of devil-worshipers.

Serpent: Symbol of Judgment on Sin

> And the LORD sent fiery serpents among the people, and they bit the people; and much people of Israel died. Therefore the people came to Moses, and said, We have sinned, for we have spoken

> against the LORD, and against thee; pray unto the
> LORD, that he take away the serpents from us
> (Num 21:6-7).

Here God sent fiery serpents among the people in judgment on their sin of rebellion against Him and Moses, His man. To save the people from this judgment on sin, what cure did God have?

> And the LORD said unto Moses, Make thee a fiery
> serpent, and set it upon a pole: and it shall come to
> pass, that every one that is bitten, when he looketh
> upon it, shall live. And Moses made a serpent of brass,
> and put it upon a pole, and it came to pass, that if
> a serpent had bitten any man, when he beheld the
> serpent of brass, he lived (Num 21:8-9).

This seems to be a strange thing indeed! An image of the very thing that was causing the trouble was to be hung upon a wooden shaft, and all who obeyed God and looked at that image would not die from the serpent's bite! What was the purpose of this peculiar remedy? What did it mean? Was there some deeper reason for this whole episode than what appears on the surface?

In the New Testament, Jesus gives the answer:

> And as Moses lifted up the serpent in the wilderness,
> even so must the Son of man be lifted up: that
> whosoever believeth in him should not perish, but
> have eternal life (Jn 3:14-15).

Here, some time before Jesus Christ was crucified, He predicted His crucifixion to one of the greatest religious leaders of Israel, Nicodemus. Jesus even took this occasion to explain the true symbolic meaning of the serpent in the wilderness.

Immediately the thought arises, "But if the serpent is symbolic of sin or of God's judgment on sin, how then can it be symbolic of Jesus on the cross?"

The Scripture again is its own interpreter: "For he hath made him to be sin for us, who knew no sin; that we might be made the righteousness of God in him" (2 Co 5:21). When Jesus died on the cross, the crushing weight of the penalty and judgment of sin—of our sin—fell upon the innocent Lamb of God. This was the most horrible, excruciating pain ever to be suffered by a human being, because the perfect Son of God had to bear the awful agony of separation from His Father because of our sins. Hear Him as He cries, "My God, my God, why hast thou forsaken me?" amid the crash of thunder and splitting asunder of the rocks. "For God so loved the world, that he gave his only begotten Son, that whosoever believeth in him should not perish but have everlasting life" (Jn 3:16).

As the people in the wilderness looked up at the serpent to save them from the immediate penalty of their sin, so we must look to Jesus to save us from the ultimate penalty of our sins. It is not enough, then, for us to believe that Christ merely died on the cross as a good example, or as a martyr to a cause. When we look up there at Him on the cross, we must see Him as our sin-bearer.

Perhaps one of the sweetest, yet most heartrending portions in the Old Testament is:

> Surely he hath borne our griefs, and carried our sorrows; yet we did esteem him stricken, smitten of God,

and afflicted. But he was wounded for our transgressions, he was bruised for our iniquities: the chastisement of our peace was upon him; and with his stripes we are healed. All we like sheep have gone astray; we have turned every one to his own way; and the LORD hath laid on him the iniquity of us all (Is 53:4-6).

9

THE BIRDS

> And God said, Let the waters swarm with swarms of living creatures, and let birds fly above the earth in the open firmament of heaven. And God created the great sea-monsters, and every living creature that moveth, wherewith the waters swarmed, after their kind, and every winged bird after his kind: and God saw that it was good (Gen 1:20-21, ASV).

BEFORE MAN EVER THOUGHT about soaring through skies, birds had done it for thousands of years. Bea fully and scientifically designed for swift, lc flight, a bird has a light beak instead of heavy jaws a teeth, hollow bones that fill with air, powerful fea ered wings and breast muscles, a strong heart, an superior system of respiration. He is an amazing co bination of high power and low weight!

When man decided he would like to fly, he stud God's original fliers, the birds. Planes fly by the sa aerodynamic principles. But it took man a long ti to learn the aerodynamics built into birds by the greatest Designer of all. Planes have the same equipment as birds: wings, steering gear, slots and flaps for taking off and landing, and antistalling devices. The hummingbird is God's little "helicopter." He can poise motionless in the air, his wings beating 75 times per second, fly sideways, forward, backward, up, and down.

Barbules and barbicels on a single bird feather may number over a million! The quill is strong, elastic, tough, light, hollow, and tapers to a precision point. A bird's wing is stronger than any wing structure devised by man. Birds are the fastest creatures on our planet. A swallow, with his bones and body filled with air, can rise like a balloon and float through the air at the rate of two miles per minute or more. He can fly as much as 120 miles per hour without getting exhausted. It would only take a day and a half for a swallow to fly from New York to Europe!

The peregrine falcon can dive on prey at up to 250 miles per hour under perfect control. The African eagle diving at prey at 100 miles per hour can come to a dead halt in twenty feet! The braking power in our machines has yet to equal this.

Since it took man, with his intelligence, thousands of years to develop a flying machine, how can we by any stretch of the imagination believe that the intricate flying machine he imitated came into being by mere chance? Upon close study of an airplane, we would say, "This is the invention of a superior intelligence." Can we consistently say anything else about a bird?

Species of Birds

According to Genesis 2:21, the Lord made every bird "after his kind." There are over 9,000 species and altogether about 25,000 species and sub-species of birds.

Each species was especially made to live in its particular environment; God equipped each species especially for its needs. Egg yolk (which is body-building material), incubation, birth strength, body growth, and the molting process are all perfectly adapted for each kind of bird. A bird also is made to mature much quicker than a mammal because of his need to fly and the necessary growth of feathers in relation to body weight.

Legs and Feet

Legs and feet of various kinds were especially given for running, wading, swimming, climbing, scratching, holding, tearing, or perching. God gave the ducks paddles. To the long-legged birds (such as cranes) that stand easily on one leg, He gave legs with joints that snap into place like pocketknife blades. Leg bones of walking birds are well developed at birth. The bird that perches in trees sleeps safely and well because he has a built-in safety-lock mechanism; when his leg muscles relax, his tarsal joint automatically flexes and the toes curl up and grip the perch tighter.

Wings

Some species have great, sweeping wings, others

short, rounded wings. The wings of birds that must fly earlier are already well developed at birth, and their wing feathers grow much quicker than those of other birds. The owl is equipped with silencer equipment on his wing and tail feathers.

Beaks

Our feathered friends have beaks which can crack shells, tear prey into pieces, bore holes in trees and dig out the insects, scoop up food, pry pine cones apart, or sip nectar from flowers. Each beak was devised by God to accommodate the eating habits of its owner. Night birds, for instance, have sensitive touch organs on their beaks.

Eyes, Ears, and Radar

The eyes of birds have amazing telescopic ability to see insects or prey at a distance. Owls' eyes are ten times more sensitive to faint light than are people's. An owl also finds his food and direction in the dark by a radarlike system which involves acutely sensitive hearing. And a robin can actually hear a worm stirring in the ground.

Weatherproofing

Many birds have little purses of oil in their bodies with which to periodically waterproof themselves so they do not become sodden and heavy when they get wet. Newborn ducklings rub themselves dry under their mother, then rub against her feathers to cover their down with some of her oil. Thus they are waterproofed and can then be led out of their nests and into the water.

Evolved or Created?

To say that all these miracles of creation are merely the result of blind-chance evolution would be much like saying, "Radar came into existence by itself; airplanes, pocketknives, safety-lock mechanisms, and silencer equipment evolved from a mess of iron in the earth; telescopes and hearing aids crawled out of the sea one day to get some sun; and waterproof jackets evolved after being rained on for millions of years!"

Feeding

Birds devour an enormous amount of insects and other pests in a very short period of time, thus performing an inestimable service for mankind. One swallow will devour as many as 2,000 mosquitoes a day, as well as flies and other insects. The wren, as well as a number of other birds, will eat its weight in insects in one day.

Various species are in charge of "Operation Insect Cleanup" in different places of business. Swifts, swallows, and martins, for instance, can catch insects in their wide mouths as they fly. Woodpeckers, flycatchers, and others catch them among the trees. Birds such as sparrows get their insect meals in the bushes. Robins, meadowlarks, and others clean up the insects and worms on the ground. Sandpipers and herons take care of the insects around a lake. Often when man has destroyed birds for sport or by poisonous insecticides, trees are eaten bare by caterpillars, and crops may be eaten down to the roots.

Birds of prey keep the number of mice down. Vultures are also "God's undertakers." The secretary bird of Africa eats snakes, lizards, and scorpions. Storks feed on frogs, lizards, serpents, mice, grubs, vermin, and insects, and are also scavengers. They are very useful birds, for they clean up towns and farms; they are one branch of God's garbage men. Birds also keep weeds in check by eating weed seeds.

Woodpeckers are the only living things able to locate and eradicate the insect hordes that live under the bark of trees. One woodpecker can eat thousands of carpenter ants or other insects in a very short time. These birds locate the insects in the tree by their acute power of hearing. With the chisel-shaped tip of their beaks they penetrate the bark of the tree at the exact spot where a nest of insects is located. With the "adhesive tape" end of their long, specially made tongue, they whip into insect galleries and scour them clean of occupants.

Instincts

Although birds are low on the intelligence scale in creatures, God gave them certain instincts to make up for their lack of brains. They have the instincts to fly, to court, to propagate, to build nests, to incubate, to feed their young, and to migrate. The instinct to feed the young was given by God to all birds except those which have offspring capable of getting their own food (e.g., ducks, geese, and brush turkeys). Instinctively birds know what is the best food for their species and how to get it.

Another instinct in some birds, such as wood pigeons, partridges, plovers, and ducks, is to use the broken-wing trick to attract danger away from their broods. One of these birds will flutter to the ground and pretend his wing is broken and he is helpless. The birds that nest on or near the ground are the greatest users of this trick. Through observation it has been learned that this is done by pure instinct, not through conscious intelligence. The Lord has thus well-equipped these ground nesters to protect their vulnerable families.

Courting

The instinct to court and mate is given to all birds to a greater or lesser degree. While the cowbird has a most casual approach to mating, only barely enough to reproduce another cowbird, many birds have elaborate and fascinating courtship practices, varying with the species. Often the male will go to great pains to attract and court the female. He will even go to the trouble of weaving a beautiful delicate nest in order to attract a mate. The bower bird of Australia builds a lovely bower or hut, strewing it with pretty shells and painting it with charcoal.

Home and Family

After courtship and mating, if the nest has not already been built by the courting male, the instinct to build a home for their prospective family takes over with most birds. Without any previous experience or training, each species can build its own characteristic nest. Young birds build nests just as competently as their parents. Even though they surely do not know about the brood that is coming, they begin building their nests as egg-laying time approaches. Every individual of a species builds its nest in exactly the same way as its brothers.

Birds that build their nests in protected places usually lay few eggs. Those living under more dangerous conditions lay as many as thirty eggs. Birds that lay eggs in open nests on the ground have eggs with brown markings, and their babies are also speckled or striped for camouflage. This birth phenomenon rivals the most elaborate camouflage creation of man. These species would not have survived very long if God had not made them that way in the very beginning.

The woodpecker chisels out a deep tunnel in a tree, and his offspring have no soft nest to sit in. But God has equipped them with a special heel pad to protect them until they are able to sit up.

Some species of hummingbirds build their nests with spider webs so that the nests will expand with the growing young. The chimney swift glues his nest of twigs in a chimney or hollow tree. The kingfisher digs a tunnel in the side of a riverbank and builds his nest with the leftovers from his fish meals after he has providentially digested and regurgitated them. From man's point of view this may seem revolting, but from the baby kingfisher's view it is solid comfort.

African weavers build themselves regular gigantic apartment houses, each family having its own nest in the building. The pendulum tit builds a tightly woven sidesaddle type of nest with a side entrance which hangs precariously from a swaying poplar branch. Birds of prey, such as eagles and hawks, build huge eyries in the tops of trees or on mountain crags.

The male brush turkey builds a pile of leaves in which the female lays her eggs. Then he carefully regulates the temperature of the pile by testing its heat, then adds or scratches off leaves if necessary. While the incubator is a marvelous invention, this male turkey instinctively knows as much about proper incubation as the most scientific farmer! Surely in thousands of years his family could not have evolved such unusual wisdom. The first male brush turkey had to know just what to do, or there would never have been any more brush turkeys!

The same is true for other birds concerning incubation. In some cases the mother bird does all the work of incubating. In these cases the mother usually has a drab, unnoticeable coat, although the father may be a gaudy fellow. Many species of birds alternate the job of incubation, father and mother taking regular turns around the clock until babies are hatched. After hatching, both father and mother will work to bring food to their growing brood.

The king penguins, which are perfectly adapted to their hostile Antarctic environment, have an interesting way of taking care of their egg. Both mother and father have a special fold of belly skin and take turns sheltering the egg on their feet behind this flap. The egg is never allowed to touch the ice when transferred from parent to parent.

In some species of penguins the father sits on the eggs and goes without food for several months during the dead of winter, while the mother may be some fifty or sixty miles away getting herself well fed and ready to take over the feeding job when the babies hatch. Even though many white miles stretch between her and her family, she always finds her way over the trackless ice and snow to them in time for the hatching of her brood! While man needs keen intelligence as well as compasses, maps, radio, sounding devices, and other inventions to find his way from one place to another, this female penguin has an intuitive guidance system in both timing and direction that can only come from God.

Migration

Migration is another instinctive undertaking of birds. Many species of birds migrate hundreds or thousands of miles in the fall of the year, and in the spring they return the same distance to the same vicinity in which they had lived the year before. Often they return to the same backyard or field year after year. What compass guides them? How can they tell one air lane from another? How do they manage to return to the same country, the same state, the same county, the same city, or the same backyard year after year? Migration is a miracle of God.

The Arctic tern summers in the Arctic and winters in the Antarctic. His round trip probably runs around 22,000 miles! The golden plover makes his amazing journey from Alaska to Hawaii. More than 100 species of American birds commute to Central and South

America for their winter vacations, then return to the exact areas in the United States and Canada in which their ancestors lived (and where they were born).

The tiny German warbler leaves by itself in the fall and flies over the southern part of Europe, continuing south until it reaches its goal in southern Africa. In the spring it returns northward to Germany to set up housekeeping again. Scientific studies have revealed that these birds get their navigation from the stars.

Beauty of Birds

We cannot discuss the wonder and miracle of birds without pointing to their beauty of grace, color, and song. Have you ever admired the streamlined form of a bird soaring through the sky? Have you ever thrilled to the enchanting trills of a mocking bird? Has the beauty of a peacock or a flamingo made you wish you were a painter?

I believe that one of the reasons God made birds was to cheer the heart of man. People who think that God prefers somber colors or somber attitudes are much mistaken. All one has to do is to look around a little and see some of the beautiful creations He has made. And the birds are among the foremost.

His Eye Is on the Sparrow

The Lord Jesus Christ, when He was on earth, spoke in His Sermon on the Mount of God's care for the birds. He said, "Are not five sparrows sold for two farthings, and not one of them is forgotten before God?" (Lk 12:6). He used this illustration primarily to show God's greater concern and love for man. "But even the very hairs of your head are all numbered. Fear not therefore: ye are of more value than many sparrows" (Lk 12:7).

Yes, God knows exactly where every little sparrow is and what is happening to it, but He also knows exactly how many hairs are on your head! David said, "Thou knowest my downsitting and mine uprising." God is interested in every little phase in our lives. He also works in every life to seek to draw that one to Him. Even the atheist and agnostic have felt the tug of God at some time in their lives, but they have turned away from it. It has been truly said that "there are no atheists in foxholes."

A person who has come to know Christ as his Saviour can look back on his life and say, "Ah, yes, I remember when God sent a witness to me several years ago. I remember too when I felt the presence and attraction of God at a certain time. Yes, God worked many times in my life to draw me to Himself, to help me find His way of salvation through Christ!"

God is especially interested in those who join His family through their faith in His Son, Jesus Christ. The Bible says, "All things work together for good to them that love God, to them who are the called according to his purpose" (Ro 8:28). If every instinct is built into the birds for their welfare, how much more so is the Christian given the instinct to know and to do God's will? "For it is God which worketh in you both to will and to do of his good pleasure" (Phil 2:13).

Jesus, again showing God's love for His creation, man, said, "O Jerusalem, Jerusalem, thou that killest the prophets, and stonest them which are sent unto thee, how often would I have gathered thy children together, even as a hen gathereth her chickens under her wings, and ye would not!" (Mt 23:37). What a strikingly touching picture this is of the tender concern and patience of God! The love of God for man seems almost incomprehensible at times. Why, after Saul persecuted and helped put to death some of God's choicest saints, did God yet have mercy on him and save his soul on the Damascus Road? How, when a person has been a murderer, a harlot, or an atheistic God-denier, can God forgive him and love him enough to reveal His grace through Jesus Christ to that flagrant sinner?

The true story has been told of an agnostic who went the length and breadth of the United States, as well as all over the world, speaking against God and the Bible. Yet, when this infidel was standing on the rear platform of a train passing through one of the magnificent canyons in the western United States, he was so struck by the wonderful grandeur and immensity of it that he fell to his knees in awe, as one struck down. At that moment he knew, through the revelation of God, that there was a God. Later in London he came to a saving knowledge of Jesus Christ. This well-known lecturer changed from an infidel into a believer in a matter of a few seconds, and the rest of his life was spent in refuting his earlier teachings. God had gathered another formerly rebellious and blind chick under His wings.

"Surely he shall deliver thee from the snare of the fowler, and from the noisome pestilence. He shall cover thee with his feathers, and under his wings shalt thou trust: his truth shall be thy shield and buckler" (Ps 91:3-4). How often Christians have found comfort in this assurance from God's Word! What a blessing it is to know that we have an all-powerful God who protects us from danger and in whose keeping we can enjoy perfect peace. In His truth we have true serenity, not being buffeted about by every wind of doctrine or by the doubts, fears, and uncertainty that must surely assail the agnostic and atheist! Under His wings we are safe!

"As an eagle stirreth up her nest, fluttereth over her young, spreadeth abroad her wings, taketh them, beareth them on her wings: so the LORD alone did lead him, and there was no strange god with him" (Deu 32:11-12). Here again God uses a bird for illustration of His care and training of those who trust in Him. In order to get her young birds to fly, the eagle places pieces of glass or sharp rock in the nest, and sometimes pushes her young off the edge of the nest if the sharp objects do not induce them to take wing. Then as they hesitatingly fall off into space, the mother hovers over them, anxiously watching to see if they will fly or continue to fall.

Perhaps the first few times they do not catch on to flying. Mother eagle swoops under her falling baby and catches him on the broad sweep of her wings, bearing him back up to the nest again.

Thus God does with the new Christian, who is a babe in God's family. He is young in the faith still, and does not know quite how to walk for God in every aspect of his life. God puts sharp objects into the nest of the new Christian. These help him to grow up in the faith, in grace and knowledge of the Lord and His will. Some of the things that come into his life may cause him to slide backward (to fall as he tries to fly), but God is hovering over him as a tender mother would. As the baby starts to fall, underneath are God's everlasting wings to catch him.

The Bible says, "There hath no temptation taken you but such as is common to man: but God is faithful, who will not suffer you to be tempted above that ye are able; but will with the temptation also make a way to escape, that ye may be able to bear it" (1 Co 10:13). In other ways God can be likened to the eagle. Jesus Christ, who was God in the flesh (Jn 1:1, 14), came to earth to pay the penalty for man's sins with His own blood on the cross of Calvary. "So Christ was once offered to bear the sins of many; and unto them that look for him shall he appear the second time without sin unto salvation" (Heb 9:28).

Thus Christ took upon Himself the sins of many. The eagle is a bird covered with vermin, which are symbolic of the repulsiveness of the sins of man. Yet the eagle is a bird that soars up toward the sun. So Christ ascended to heaven and sits on the right hand of God the Father! Again the eagle is used in the Bible as an illustration of those who trust in God. When a person accepts Jesus Christ as his personal Saviour, the Spirit of Christ comes to dwell in him, and he becomes part of Christ's spiritual body, the Church. He is identified with God and Christ in a unique way.

Isaiah says, "But they that wait upon the LORD shall renew their strength; they shall mount up with wings as eagles; they shall run, and not be weary; and they shall walk, and not faint" (40:31). When a person first accepts Christ as his Saviour, he is caught up with rapture at the thrill and joy of really knowing God for the first time in his life. He is spiritually soaring in his newfound faith. He almost walks on air.

When my husband accepted Christ, his heart was flooded with joy. He wanted to tell everyone about what Christ had done for him. When people would ask him questions about the Bible or his faith, Al would open the Bible. It seemed as if the Bible always turned open to the right page with the right verse to answer. After he had been the Lord's for a while, however, he found that the Lord expected him to learn the Bible for himself and to be able to answer from his own knowledge of it.

The same thrilling joy fills a person who has come back to Christ after going astray, or who has had his faith renewed and buoyed up through rededication or through waiting upon the Lord (studying His Word and praying). After several months the initial exuberance of salvation or rededication wears off, to be replaced by a quiet serene confidence that one belongs to Christ. There is still an excited flurry of activity and witnessing for the Lord that can be likened to running and not being weary, even when the person meets rebuke after rebuke because of his zealous—and sometimes not too wise—witnessing.

After I made Christ the Lord of my life I rashly witnessed for the Lord in what I now realize was an offensive way, for I greatly antagonized several whom I yearned to see come to Christ. Eventually one of the two I had greatly offended did come to Christ, but not before I had abjectly humbled myself to both her and another person, apologizing profusely for upsetting them so. I realize now that much of my witnessing in my early Christian days was "in the flesh," not "according to the Spirit." I was running and not taking time enough to see the will of the Lord in my running!

"Walking and not fainting" is perhaps the hardest of all three things that a Christian must do. Mounting up on wings as eagles is not hard; it is automatic! It comes as natural as breathing. To run and not be weary is no great task when one is still young in the Lord, still fired with great energy for His cause of winning souls and trying to live for Him. But the "walking and not fainting" depends on a constant, day-by-day communion with God after the Christian has reached spiritual adulthood.

There are many Christians who are still in the babyhood of being a Christian. They never get past the flying stage. That is, when they come to Christ, they fly for a short while, then fall back to the nest, stones and all. Then they go to a good revival meeting, rededicate themselves, fly for another short while, but fall back again! Their lives are a terrible inconsistency. They are the ones that people look at and say, "If that's a Christian, I don't want to be one!"

The second kind of Christian is almost as bad. He is the one who has reached the running stage but has never developed beyond that. He runs here, he runs there, seeking to serve the Lord in the energy of his flesh, but not by the leading of the Holy Spirit. He thinks his "Martha" way is the most pleasing to God, and that more is accomplished in that way than in any other. But Jesus says to him, "Mary hath chosen the better part." Actually many people are driven *from* the Lord by this type of person. He is acting so much in the flesh that he tries to force people to make "decisions for Christ" before they have been made ready by the Holy Spirit. Sometimes he confuses legality with salvation, hammering away on unsaved people by telling them that they must do or give up certain things as well as come to Jesus.

Thus an actual blockade to coming to Christ is set up in the minds of people, and they think that Christ will not accept them as long as they do certain things. They therefore may try to perfect themselves before coming to Christ, which is an actual impossibility! Or else they continue on in their way of life and believe they cannot be saved because they are not good enough. In any case, they have been sadly misled, for they never will have either the power or inclination to become a godly person until they do receive Christ as their Saviour.

Now there is nothing wrong with "running" as far as the fairly new Christian is concerned; it is as natural a part of his growth as it is for a nine-year-old boy to run. But when that nine-year-old boy grows up and still acts like a nine-year-old, then something is wrong. His development has been stunted. The Bible calls the stunted Christian a "carnal Christian." This person gives rise to the havoc that is created in churches at times; he is a source of division, a creator of cliques (1 Co 3:1-3).

He needs to start really "waiting upon the Lord,"

spending time with the Lord as Mary did, sitting quietly at His feet and learning. Then he will begin to develop into a spiritual Christian, one who walks day by day with Christ, one who does not fluctuate as much as he who flies or runs. Now he will become the kind of Christian who looks to the Lord for guidance in everything he does in his personal or church life. Now the Christ life in him will begin to really shine out, and others will see Christ in him. A hunger to know God will stir in the hearts of many with whom he comes in contact.

Enoch was a man who "walked with God." We too can have this precious privilege by drawing nigh unto God, by dedicating our lives to His service, and by waiting upon Him for His guidance and direction. Through daily devotional times, through faithful attendance at church services, and through faithful obedience to His revealed will, we too may "walk with God."

10

BEASTS OF THE FIELD

> For every beast of the forest is mine, and the cattle upon a thousand hills (Ps 50:10).

> Who knoweth the spirit of man that goeth upward, and the spirit of the beast that goeth downward to the earth? (Ec 3:21).

THE HAIRY APE swings down from the tree limb grunting and scratching himself. A human mother, standing with her young son on the other side of the bars, looks in at him and laughs. "There," she says to her five-year-old, "is one of your relatives!" The boy looks at the ape in puzzlement, but says nothing. His education in evolution has unwittingly been started by his own whimsical mother.

In perhaps the third or fourth grade this education is continued with seriousness by impressive-speaking teachers who honestly believe in the theory. Yet, the ape differs so very greatly from man, it is hard to believe that so many educated people can accept the belief that their ancestors came from a creature similar to this grotesque beast! Long arms, no chin, and canine teeth are just a few of the things in which the ape differs from us. There are, in fact, thousands of vital differences between ape and man, and there is not a creature in existence that bridges the tremendous gap.

The ape does not have opposable thumbs as man does; thus, he is completely unable to handle tools and manipulate the many wonderful things that man uses to make life better for himself.

The ape's brain lacks the vital speech area that was planted in man's brain by God. Without that speech area, man would never be capable of conversing. Again, if there were any link between ape and man, we would expect some apes to have this area and some men to be born without it.

An ape's hind feet have thumbs; man's feet are built for walking and running and are entirely different from his hands. Apes have never known how to use fire, but wherever there is an archaeological record of man, there is evidence of his charcoal fires. Apes plant no gardens and grow no food, yet even tiny ants have farms and cattle which they tend fastidiously.

Apes neither laugh nor cry nor worship. Yet man has the tender emotions planted in his heart by God that give him tears and grief, joy and happiness, sympathy and kindness, that cause him to turn his eyes Godward. All these things reflect the fact that he was "made in the image of God."

God's Balance in Nature

Each species of animal has a purpose in life; each one is a part of God's balance in nature. Man has found that whenever he has tampered with God's distribution of creatures and plants, something goes haywire. All animals are completely and beautifully equipped to live in their particular environment.

Instinct and Intelligence

Many animals seem to have uncanny intelligence, but most of it can be attributed to the wonderful instincts that God has built into them for their preservation and usefulness. Among their most valuable instincts are those which warn them of imminent danger, help them tell a friend from foe, make them aware of fear in an opponent, and help them to know what to do in many situations. This last one applies to a wide category which includes obtaining food, home-building, courtship and family life, and community responsibility.

For instance, in home-building, chipmunks always remove the dirt they dig out when making their burrows. By making new exits to their burrows, they are able to go back to the original hole and close it up with the telltale dirt, scattering the remainder of the dirt all around. Thus the entrances to their homes are safe from their enemies. Since their brain capacity certainly is not great enough to figure all this out, it stands to reason that someone endowed each little chipmunk with a built-in behavior track so that he knows just what to do every time.

Woodchucks have been known to thrust a fractured leg into mud, and the mud then hardens into a sort of cast. Other animals plaster their wounds with leaves, mud, plant down, etc., thus providing a covering for them until they heal. Instinctively animals lick and suck their wounds, licking and drawing out the germs and poisons in them.

Senses

Most animals have excellent nighttime vision. God has built reflectors into their eyes in order to collect the dim light in which they do their hunting and prowling. That is why their eyes seem to shine so at night. On the other hand, to protect their eyes during the daytime, some of them have been given slit pupils which they can narrow at will (like a shutter lens on a camera).

Animals also have excellent hearing, for their lives often depend on it. A dog can hear something a mile away that a man could hear only 175 yards away. Dogs also have such a fine discernment of difference between musical notes that they can actually distinguish between two tones almost exactly alike. They, as well as other animals, can tell exactly from where a sound is coming. The sense of smell is acute and highly developed in animals. They depend on it not only to find food, but also to find mates. Animals will map out with their scents the area of their particular domain, and other animals get the message with their noses.

Mouths: Eating Equipment

Since animals do not have hands with which to bring food to their mouths, they are equipped with special mouths. The sheep, the horse, and the ox, which need to browse on pasture, have full lips, rough tongues, broad cutting teeth, and furrowed flexible palates. Thus not only can they gather in large grasses, but also bite close on short grass.

The pig has a prong for an underjaw which works with his snout to dig out the desired roots for his diet. The dog has projecting jaws and pointed teeth with which he is able to snatch and seize his prey or food.

The elephant has a long proboscis which enables him with his short neck and long pillarlike legs to pick up his food and eat it, to drink water, and to take a shower bath. There are 20,000 muscles in this versatile appendage.

Fur Coats

All mammals have fur or hair. Dense fur keeps the body heat from escaping and protects against injury and cold. Animals living in cold climates have thick coats of fur. That is why fur traders will go far north into Canada to buy fine furs. In warm seasons furred animals conveniently shed some of their hair because they do not need so much "insulation." Animals that do not take to the water have their thickest fur on top. Those that do, such as the beaver, have a much thicker coat on their abdominal areas than on their backs.

Most animals are colored to blend in with their surroundings, so they are protected by camouflage.

Tigers and lions have mottled, striped, or tawny fur that blends in beautifully with surrounding foliage. The backs of spotted fawn are darker than their underparts in order to counterbalance the effects of lighting and shadows. Sloths are colored in exactly the opposite manner because they live hanging upside down. They are further colored to blend with their surroundings by an interesting green alga that lives on them.

Snowshoe rabbits, northern weasels, and arctic foxes wear convenient white coats in the winter in order to blend in with the snow. In the spring they shed these white coats and grow new brown or tawny coats for their summer surroundings. Thus God has provided them with perfect camouflage. This is indeed a strange and yet too consistent thing to ever have evolved.

Tails

Tails serve animals as chairs, extra hands, signals, instruments of communication, weapons, fly swatters, and tools of many uses. The kangaroo props himself on his tail and relaxes. Beavers use their tails to sound "whomping" alarm signals to other beavers and to sit on while gnawing trees down; they also use them as swimming rudders. Mice use their tails as dippers to reach food in inaccessible places.

Bushy tails are handy accessories also. The busy tail of the winter fox serves him well as a wraparound to keep his nose warm on frosty nights. The squirrel uses his bushy tail as a steering rudder for jumps and a balancing parasol for walking on small limbs. It also serves as a fine parachute when he misses or misjudges his target and falls.

Hibernation

Woodchucks, chipmunks, bats, and bears, as well as certain ground squirrels, go into a period of hibernation during the winter months. With the exception of bears, there is a slowing down of all their natural bodily processes. Padded with fat, these animals crawl into their burrows or caves and fall into a deep unconsciousness until the hibernation period is over. This is one of God's provisions to tide these animals over during a period of food scarcity, and it is truly a miracle in nature.

Radar

During World War II radar was top secret by our government, for it was a newly discovered, extremely valuable protective device. But this wonderful thing that mankind did not discover until the twentieth century has been guiding bats around ever since they came into existence.

Emitting bursts of sound in frequencies up to 32,000 per second, they fly unerringly through darkest night or cave without colliding with anything. As their high-pitched squeaks bounce back from various obstacles, the bats change their courses to avoid these obstacles. Even though there may be hundreds of bats flying in and out of a cave, each bat is able to guide himself by his own signals. A bat can catch hundreds of tiny insects in an hour with his amazingly accurate radar system.

FAMILY LIFE

God gives animals every little instinct they need in order to do the right thing as parents, and as newborn babes.

A male coyote is a "family man." He eloquently courts his mate, then is an excellent father and husband. He not only provides for his family, but also protects them, even to the extent that he will make a decoy of himself to draw trouble away from his family. He has an excellent memory and will remember experiences in his past that might save his life in the future. He is a valuable balance in nature, for he keeps down the population of the pesky jackrabbits which devour men's crops.

When kangaroo babies are born they are only one-inch long. But they know instinctively what to do. Scrabbling through mother's fur until they come to her pouch, they go into the warm pocket and latch tenaciously onto a milk fountain there. From then on mother's milk is pumped automatically into baby, for the baby is too small and weak to help himself. It is a wonder how a little thing only an inch long can find its way to the right place. It is marvelous that long before mankind devised the automatic milking machine, the kangaroo had such a perfect device. This flesh-and-blood automatic milk pumper had to have a Creator just as much as our electric milk pumper did!

Three elephant midwives excitedly attended the birth in Portland, Oregon, of one of the few baby elephants ever to be born in captivity. The mother Belle's God-given maternity instinct came into action even as her 225-pound infant dropped quietly to the floor in a heap. She swiftly knotted or clamped the umbilical stump with her trunk. She gave her newborn son a few swift kicks in his fuzzy flanks and slowly but firmly he arose on his stout little legs. Shoving him gently with her forelegs and trunk, Belle nudged her baby's head around to her breast. The baby knew what to do when he got there.

Animals in many cases actually train their children better than humans do, because they discipline them well and teach them obedience. They also train them in the way they should live. Mother bears train their cubs to be quiet for safety's sake by growling at them or cuffing them when they get noisy. Mother otters and sea lions teach their babies to swim by taking them out into the water on their backs and then ducking out from under them.

Since human parents have far more intelligence than animal parents, we must conclude that the instincts God gives animals to train their children, and which they unerringly obey, are better by far than the man with wisdom who leaves a child to his own devices.

USEFUL ANIMALS

Animals serve many useful purposes in God's economy for this world. People who like to eat some kind of meat each day might find it a pretty drab existence if they did not have cattle, sheep, and pigs to provide them with these meats. Since many babies today are bottle fed instead of in the natural way, most modern mothers would be lost without cows' milk.

For that matter, cows' milk provides us with the most outstanding source of food and nutrition today.

For centuries oxen, asses, mules, and horses have been beasts of burden, helping man with his plowing, his herding, and his traveling. Dogs too have been a big help to man by tending, protecting, and rounding up herds of cattle and sheep.

The squirrel is God's little nut-tree planter.

WALKING WATER TANKS

The camel is man's beast of burden for the desert. God even gave the camel pads on his knees to equip him for this purpose. In his hump are fatty deposits that tide him over for long trips between food. His paunch contains around 800 little water flasks which are filled up at oases to make it possible for him to go across the desert for several weeks without water.

The camel has built-in wind glasses, transparent third eyelids which protect his eyes against the whirling sands during violent desert storms. He has amazing durability and can travel great distances without rest. And he also supplies his owner with food and clothing. What a wonderful special creation the camel is!

THE DAM BUILDERS

Beavers are God's water conservationists and engineers. They built dams long before mankind ever thought about it. And undoubtedly it was through man's observation of the beavers' works that dams were first built by man. Beavers skillfully build remarkable dams, sometimes more than 150 yards across, to form large pools of water and even lakes. They build themselves a lodge with storage chambers on this dam. Not only they, but many other creatures, find a home and safety in this construction.

When beavers need more timber for their construction, they build canals inland several hundred feet to safely float the trees to their dam. When large numbers of beavers were killed off in a certain part of Canada, it seriously affected the economy of the whole area. Severe droughts set in and men, animals, and fish suffered or died because of the water shortages. Beavers were brought in from other areas in order to restore the natural resources to this drought-stricken place.

Cats: All Kinds

Cats are beautifully built animals and have many things about their structure that prove the workmanship of an intelligent Creator. Especially strong and sharp teeth are provided for these carnivorous animals. Large fangs near the front of their mouths act as daggers for stabbing prey and holding it. Their tongues, too, are just right for them. They use them for tasting, testing, and rasping food off before and after the teeth are used. They are very handy fur cleaners and are also formed into shallow cups. Thus the cats are able to scoop water into their mouths.

Since a cat's life usually depends on his claws, God built special little pouches in the feet where the claws can be withdrawn when not in use. In this way they are not blunted by walking as a dog's are. A cat's claws are also stacked into sharply pointed curved cones that fit one inside another so that when the outer one is worn or broken, it is shed and a new, sharp claw exposed.

Another thing that a cat depends on is his hearing, which is far more acute than man's. A cat can tell exactly from where a sound is coming by moving his ears around like radar gear. Cats are color-blind, but here again the provisional hand of God is seen. This color-blindness enables a cat to see prey which would otherwise be camouflaged among varicolored foliage. Cats have excellent nighttime vision with which they are able to detect the faintest light or reflection of light. To protect their sensitive eyes during the daytime, they have a special muscle (just as other animals and men do) which contracts their pupils so that less light can enter. A night-hunting cat's pupil, however, is shaped like a football and can therefore contract much further than man's round eye. Day-hunting cats have a conventional round pupil.

If anyone has ever watched a litter of kittens being born, he knows that the wondrous instinct in both mother and kittens to do just the right thing is surely a God-given phenomenon.

THE HORSE

The horse has a splint bone in each leg that forms a sort of brace, thus giving him remarkable speed and stamina in flight. His leg joints automatically lock into place when he goes to sleep, affording him perfect comfort and rest. Man has invented various devices that use the same principle.

The horse, in evolutionist teaching, is their prime example of the proof of evolution. With twelve links in the chain, they start with the tiny Eohippus (smaller than a house cat) which was found on the American continent, and end with a regulation horse, which originally came from Europe, Asia, and Africa. Even though there should be a million valid links necessary to prove any connection between the first creature in this chain (which looked more like a civet cat) and the present horse, there are only eleven questionable fossils usable for the theory on which to build the major example of evolution in animals.

These twelve links also hop and skip from one continent to another. Several of them are purely American fossils and have never been found on the European continent. Two of them have never been found any other place outside of South America. A fossil form of a horse that once weighed three tons has been left out of this evolutionist line of horses because he did not fit the theory; he weighed two tons more than the modern horse. Many other horse fossils have been left out of the line because their inclusion would cause embarrassment to the promoters of the evolutionist theory.

Symbolical Animals

> All we like sheep have gone astray; we have turned every one to his own way; and the LORD hath laid on him the iniquity of us all. I am the good shepherd: the good shepherd giveth his life for the sheep (Is 53:6; Jn 10:11).

The Bible is rich in the use of animals to symbolize

or illustrate. Ezekiel saw four creatures in a vision with the likenesses of a lion, an ox, a man, and an eagle. These blend in so well with the unique portrayals painted of the Lord Jesus Christ in the four gospels that there can be little doubt of the relationship between the two.

The Gospel of Matthew presents Jesus Christ as the Messianic King, of which the lion is surely the symbol; Jesus is called "the Lion of the Tribe of Juda" (Rev 5:5). The Gospel of Mark presents Jesus Christ as the Servant of mankind, of which the ox is very symbolic. The Gospel of Luke presents Jesus Christ as the Son of man, and certainly man is the symbol. The Gospel of John presents Jesus Christ as the Son of God, of whom the eagle is symbolic.

The devil has two fine descriptive names given him which are most apt:

> And the great dragon was cast out, that old serpent, called the Devil, and Satan, which deceiveth the whole world: he was cast out into the earth, and his angels were cast out with him (Rev 12:9).

Dogs are symbolically used to depict people who do not want the truth of God. They not only turn from the truth, but also they despise all who truly love and know the Lord and will do all in their power to hurt them and to lead them astray. In the Old Testament days prowling dogs would go about seeking newly dead people or animals to devour. So they would seem to well depict people who choose the way of death rather than the way of life.

Wolves are also symbolic of people who not only secretly hate God and God's people, but also make it their life's work to destroy God's work and wreak havoc among His people. Jesus said, "Beware of false prophets, which come to you in sheep's clothing, but inwardly they are ravening wolves" (Mt 7:15).

The apostle Paul said, "For I know this, that after my departing shall grievous wolves enter in among you, not sparing the flock. Also of your own selves shall men arise, speaking perverse things, to draw away disciples after them" (Ac 20:29-30). Those who do not accept Christ as their personal Saviour are also likened to goats by Jesus, perhaps because goats are so cantankerous and like to eat trash. Jesus predicted that when He comes in glory and judgment, all nations shall be gathered together before Him "and he shall separate them one from another, as a shepherd divideth his sheep from the goats" (Mt 25:32).

Perhaps the most beautiful illustration in the Bible is that which likens the Lord to a good shepherd and His people to sheep. In the Old Testament, David by inspiration sang, "The LORD is my shepherd; I shall not want" (Ps 23:1).

Isaiah, presenting the other side, said, "All we like sheep have gone astray; we have turned every one to his own way; and the LORD hath laid on him the iniquity of us all" (Is 53:6).

In the New Testament Jesus said, "I am the good shepherd: the good shepherd giveth his life for the sheep. My sheep hear my voice, and I know them, and they follow me: and I give unto them eternal life; and they shall never perish, neither shall any man pluck them out of my hand" (Jn 10:11, 27-28).

The apostle Peter said, "For ye were as sheep going

astray; but are now returned unto the Shepherd and Bishop of your souls" (1 Pe 2:25). Jesus as the Good Shepherd reveals the tender loving care and concern that God has for the people of His creation. A good shepherd usually knows every one of his sheep by name; he carefully makes sure that each one is safely in the sheepfold at night. Jesus gave us the beautiful story of the good shepherd seeking one lost sheep that we might realize His concern for the salvation of even one lost soul.

Again, in identification with mankind, in that He Himself became a man, Jesus was called "the Lamb of God." More than the identification, however, was the fact that it was only through the shed blood of a lamb that atonement could be made for the sins of the people of Israel. This provision was made in the laws given by God to Moses and foreshadowed the death of God's perfect atonement for sin, Jesus Christ.

When God brought judgment on the firstborn of Egypt, He told the children of Israel to put the blood of a lamb on every one of their doorposts, so that when the angel of death passed through the land, he would pass over the children of Israel. This was symbolic of the fact that when God looks at the heart of every individual person in the world, He spares those who are washed in the blood of the Lamb from eternal death and damnation.

John the Baptist declared of Jesus, "Behold the Lamb of God, who taketh away the sin of the world." The prophet Isaiah also likened Christ, the sin-bearer, to a lamb:

He was oppressed, and he was afflicted, yet he opened

not his mouth: he is brought as a lamb to the slaughter, and as a sheep before her shearers is dumb, so he opened not his mouth (Is 53:7).

Peter confirmed this likeness:

> Forasmuch as ye know that ye were not redeemed with corruptible things, as silver and gold, from your vain conversation received by tradition from your fathers; but with the precious blood of Christ, as of a lamb without blemish and without spot (1 Pe 1:18-19).

Someday soon Jesus Christ will come to earth to reign as King. Then the world of animals will be released from the savage devilish world in which they live now:

> The wolf also shall dwell with the lamb, and the leopard shall lie down with the kid; and the calf and the young lion and the fatling together; and a little child shall lead them. And the cow and the bear shall feed; their young ones shall lie down together: and the lion shall eat straw like the ox (Is 11:6-7).

11

THE MIRACLE OF MANKIND

> And God said, Let us make man in our image, after our likeness: and let them have dominion over the fish of the sea, and over the fowl of the air, and over the cattle, and over all the earth, and over every creeping thing that creepeth upon the earth. So God created man in his own image, in the image of God created he him; male and female created he them (Gen 1:26-27).

A TINY BABY—a human being—has come into the world. On each tiny hand are four tiny fingers and an opposable thumb. With these fingers and thumbs he will be able to grasp things, hold them, move them about; play musical instruments; write down his thoughts; create beautiful works of art; use tools to build buildings and machines; dress and feed himself; play games, sew, wash things; and do a multitude of other things that no lower creature can manage.

Look at the sweet, tiny face now. Two blue eyes

look up, not three. That is all any normal human ever had. These two eyes are masterpieces of intricate design. The lenses, the irises, the corneas, the muscles, the cones: all are part of a mechanism that carries images and colors back to the brain. Through the study and knowledge of the eye, men have been able to devise complex cameras to take pictures much as the eye does.

A nose is on that wee face too; two little holes go up that nose, and through them the baby breathes oxygen. The oxygen goes down to his lungs and is circulated in his body. It is necessary not only for his life, but also for his intelligence. Of course the baby can breathe through his mouth, but God gave him this specialized nose through which the dust-laden air is filtered. When the air comes through the nose, it does not get dry as the mouth does and the taste buds are not annoyed. It can still perform the task of supplying the body with oxygen when the mouth is filled with food.

The tender, rosebud mouth opens in a cry. What a marvelous and useful thing is that mouth! Into it goes the food that will keep this human being alive. Out of it come cries at first, to notify the proper people of the needs of this new little person. Later, words start to form, aided and abetted by the tongue, palate, and voice box, all cooperating wonderfully to produce intelligible sound, melodic cadences. One wonders, according to the theory of evolution, which of these cooperative organs came into being first, or how they came into existence at all without a supreme intelligence behind their invention. It would be like a hi-fi set coming into existence in an explosion of an electronics factory!

There are just the right number of teeth that come out of the gums at just the right time. Baby does not have any in evidence to start with, for his tender little stomach just calls for the milk that came into his mother's breast for his personal use. As he grows stronger and his body demands more food, the first teeth start coming in, just enough to handle the soft food that will be given to him and that his yet tender stomach can abide. The little teeth fill in a limited space and just meet the need of the small body. As the head and face of the child grow larger, these teeth fall out, and larger, more efficient ones take their place to provide the chewing power this future adult will need.

On baby's little head is a mass of fine hairs. The hair of each individual in the world follows a distinctive pattern, set by the scales, the cortex, and the medulla. Each person's hair is as especially his as his fingerprints. Jesus said that the very hairs on a person's head are numbered! (Mt 10:30).

The baby has a stomach to digest the food for his body. He has a liver and kidneys to cleanse his body and dispose of the wastes. He has a heart to send fresh blood surging into his arteries on its way to every part of his body. He has lungs to supply that blood with the vital oxygen. He has nerves and a spinal cord to carry messages to and from his brain for the rest of his person. He has blood vessels and an intricate defense mechanism set up in his system to combat disease and infection. He has skin, hair, and nails to protect his exterior surfaces. He has bones, joints, and muscles to facilitate his bodily movement. He has organs with which to propagate his kind. He has feet to take him where he wants to go.

This little fellow has a brain and a will of his own, which parents find out very quickly! Someday he may solve profound mathematical problems, invent a new type of space fuel, speak three or four different languages, or make important decisions that will affect many others. He may learn to play a musical instrument, write challenging theses or books, or pass legislation that will have far-reaching effects on his country.

He has a soul too. As he grows older his crying will have more meaning. It will be the pouring out of a heartbroken soul. He may love a beautiful young girl; he may hate her drunken father who mistreats her. His soul may be filled with anger at injustices, with sorrow on sad occasions, with pity for those less fortunate than he. His soul will be filled with joy when his first child comes into the world; it will be filled with anguish when that precious child has his first high fever.

He will have feelings of frustration when he does not achieve some cherished goal. He will show gratitude and ingratitude, goodwill and envy, patriotism, fidelity, curiosity, and romance. He will have the esthetic nature that enables man alone to appreciate and enjoy beauty, music, and art. And there are the motivations of ambition that will encourage him to do important, worthwhile things in life.

This man child is basically a moral being. He has a

conscience, which is something no other creature possesses. He instinctively knows the difference between good and evil and has the will to choose between them. Wherever men have come under the influence of the Bible and true Christianity there has been a marked improvement in their behavior toward one another and in their subsequent living conditions. That is one reason why our United States is such a wonderful place to live.

This human being, unique in God's creation, has a spiritual nature. Created in God's image (Gen 1:27), he was made with the innate consciousness of the existence of his Creator. In Acts 17:23 Paul observes that even the idolatrous Athenians had an altar "TO THE UNKNOWN GOD." As he proceeded to declare this God who created all things, he reminded them that their own poets also spoke of Him, saying, "For we are also his offspring."

The spirit of man, however, was separated from God when man sinned. (And only men and angels can "sin.") This separation from God was perpetrated in the race of man that Adam fathered. The sin principle is born into every human being sired by a human father. God, then, in Jesus Christ, came to earth by being born of a virgin. He lived a perfect sinless life as a man and was thus able to bridge the gap between Himself and mankind by His atoning sacrifice of sinless blood.

> Therefore as by the offence of one judgment came upon all men to condemnation; even so by the righteousness of one the free gift came upon all men unto justification of life. For as by one man's disobedience

many were made sinners, so by the obedience of one shall many be made righteous (Ro 5:18-19).

When a person accepts Jesus Christ as his personal Saviour from sin, he is immediately reconciled to God and born into God's family through the Holy Spirit. Thus his spirit is restored to its rightful status and he inherits the eternal life God intended man to have.

Man's Wonderful Body

I will praise thee; for I am fearfully and wonderfully made: marvellous are thy works; and that my soul knoweth right well. Thine eyes did see my substance, yet being unperfect; and in thy book all my members were written, which in continuance were fashioned, when as yet there was none of them. How precious also are thy thoughts unto me, O God! How great is the sum of them! (Ps 139:14, 16-17).

While the other creatures we have looked at already have truly given evidence of the creative hand of God, man is undoubtedly the highest creation on earth. In his body there are some 5,000 named anatomical structures and 100,000 different kinds of protein molecules. Lord Herbert said, "Whoever considers the study of anatomy will never be an atheist. I hold it to be the greatest miracle in nature."

Let us look at this extraordinary body in detail and then at the physical thing in which man differs most from all other creatures: his brain.

The Framework: "Dem Bones"

The shape of man's body makes him the only creature that can truly be said to look Godward. He alone walks upright and can lift his face to heaven. The way his skeleton and bones are made gives him great strength with comparatively little bone weight. There are 206 bones, and every one in just the right place. Who put them there, or did they all get that way by chance? I am not a mathematician, but I wonder what the odds would be that all 206 bones would by chance grow to just the right length and be in just the right place. And what about the marvelous way in which these bones are jointed so that a person can move them in so many different ways, at the direction of his brain? Why are vital spots such as the brain, the heart, and the lungs, protected by very special bones?

Every bone in our bodies was designed for a special purpose. Our leg bones were made hollow, for hollow columns are stronger than solid ones. They are filled with bone-forming marrow. Our arms and legs can move in almost every direction because of their wonderful ball-and-socket design. Our joints are connected by strong ligaments. Our backbones and ribs form a framework that encircles many of the vital organs of our bodies.

The Skin

The skin, the hardy covering of the body, performs a great many services for us. It is the principal organ of touch, conveying to us the feelings of heat, cold, pain, pressure, and tickling. It regulates the temperature of the body. It insulates the body from heat and cold. It eliminates poisons through the sweat glands, but it is waterproof. The skin shields from overexposure to the sun by the manufacture of "melanin" which tans us. It manufactures new nails, hair, and cells. It protects us from the elements, chemicals, germs, and bacteria, and it provides an armor for the tissues of our bodies. It is a veritable storehouse for sugar, salts, water, fats, and other materials. It repairs itself.

MUSCLES

There are over 400 different muscles that aid the movements of and in our bodies. Some of these work as the result of our wills. Many work involuntarily, performing vital tasks for us constantly without any conscious effort on our part. The heart muscle is probably the most outstanding and intricate of those that work involuntarily and faithfully. It is a grand and tremendously strong pump that usually outlasts any man-made pump.

Man's splendid muscular coordination is evident in the thousands of useful and interesting things he can do. Think of what it would be like without the musician, the artist, the surgeon, the athlete, the machinist, the typist. These skills, to a refined degree, are man's and man's alone!

THE BLOOD : OUR CIRCULATION SYSTEM

"[God] hath made of one blood all nations of men for to dwell on all the face of the earth" (Ac 17:26).

The above statement was made by inspiration by the apostle Paul 2,000 years ago. Yet, only recently has this truth been proved by the science of men. We know now that regardless of what color a man's skin may be—white, black, brown, or yellow—he is able to have a blood transfusion from someone of any other race. Even the blood types do not go according to one color of skin, for people of every color have, for instance, type O blood. The blood of beasts, however, is distinctly different and cannot possibly be used for blood transfusions to men.

Some 4,000 years ago the prophet Moses by inspiration wrote: "The life of all flesh is the blood thereof." Today our biologists know it is true, but certainly a man living 4,000 years ago could not have known it to be so without the inspiration of God! In fact, until recent times physicians leeched blood out of people in trying to save their lives. Blood plasma is pumped through the arteries of our body by the most efficient pump ever made, the heart. This pump takes an amazing amount of strain and work. It is a good thing God made it such a strong organ, for it does an unbelievable amount of work!

The blood moves freely throughout our whole body, supplying it with nourishment, resistance to disease, and garbage disposal service. Every twenty-three seconds the five quarts of blood in one's body circulate through his entire system so that every cell in the body is constantly supplied and cleansed. To say that our blood and circulation systems were not the invention of God's intelligence would be somewhat like saying an automat, a hospital, and a vacuum cleaner evolved by chance.

Various precious ingredients of the blood are made by a series of complicated chemical stages in complex chemical laboratories located all over our bodies. In some aged people these little labs have worked faithfully for eighty or ninety years without a bit of direction from their owners. In fact, all of our circulation system was made by God to function automatically from the beginning to end of life.

The red cells of the blood carry the fuel of fresh oxygen to various tissues. They pick up the waste products of these tissues and carry them to discarding organs such as the kidneys, bowels, and lungs. And just think, this whole process takes only twenty-three seconds! The white cells are the "combat crew" and protect the body against the invasion of germs and disease. They also dispose of unwanted chemicals, foreign materials, and waste. Their manufacture is greatly stepped up when a messenger comes to report an invasion. A host of them races to the danger spot to kill the invading germs and engulf them. After the battle is over, these same handy little fellows clean up the battlefield and build new tissue.

Since "the life of the flesh is in the blood," God's way of salvation, of eternal life, is also centered in the blood. Leviticus 17:11 says: "And I have given it to you upon the altar to make an atonement for your souls: for it is the blood that maketh an atonement for the soul."

The sacrificial blood-atonement system of the Old Testament times was a symbolic looking forward to the day when God would provide the perfect sacrifice, "a Lamb without blemish," Jesus Christ, His Son. The Bible says:

> God commendeth his love toward us, in that, while we were yet sinners, Christ died for us. Much more then, being now justified by his blood, we shall be saved from wrath through him (Ro 5:8-9).

Just as our blood protects our bodies in times of danger and attack, so the blood of Jesus Christ protects and strengthens our minds, souls, and spirits from demonic enemies of the spiritual world.

> And I heard a loud voice saying in heaven, Now is come salvation, and strength, and the kingdom of our God, and the power of his Christ: for the accuser of our brethren is cast down, which accused them before our God day and night. And they overcame him by the blood of the Lamb and by the word of their testimony (Rev 12:10-11).

Just as our blood constantly cleanses our bodies of waste, so the blood of Christ constantly cleanses the Christian of sin:

> If we walk in the light, as he is in the light, we have fellowship one with another, and the blood of Jesus Christ his Son cleanseth us from all sin (1 Jn 1:7).

DIGESTIVE SYSTEM

The digestive system is another great system that does most of its work automatically. As food enters our mouths, the saliva glands start the process of digestion. Built into these food entrances of ours is a powerful set of biters, tearers, grinders, and chewers which we call teeth. Every human being is equipped with two sets of these remarkable gadgets, and they send well-masticated food down to his stomach.

Also built into the mouth is our versatile tongue. Not only is it our delightful organ of taste, covered with thousands of taste buds, but also it aids in the chewing and swallowing of our food properly. It is an essential organ of speech as well, working with our lips, teeth, and palate to form words. When food enters the mouth and starts on its way to the stomach, the trapdoor to the windpipe quickly closes and the food heads in the right direction through the esophagus. The esophagus, in turn, moves the food along to the stomach by muscular contractions.

Each person's stomach has at least 35 million glands which secrete various fluids and acids. These fluids not only aid in the digestion of food but also dissolve insoluble minerals and kill large numbers of bacteria that enter with the food. The stomach also contains three layers of muscles which contract in different directions to aid the stomach in its work.

After the food is churned for several hours to break it up and mix it with the secretions, the stomach valve opens at intervals and the food continues its journey on through the small intestine. Here further secretions from the liver and pancreas go to work on the food to bring about the chemical changes in the food necessary for its absorption into the body. While the food is in the small intestine, it is thus absorbed into the body through villi; then blood and lymph receive the digested food and carry it all over the body. Undigested food continues on down the small intestine to the large intestine for disposal.

Excretory System: Waste Disposal

Through the large intestine, kidneys, liver, lungs, and skin the body disposes of its waste products. The large intestine and liver work together for the disposal of solid wastes. The liver is a truly remarkable organ. Although it looks like a shapeless red brown blob, it does nineteen different jobs. It affords protection from disease, supplies sugar to meet the need of muscle tissues, turns waste nitrogen into urea for disposal, and regulates the clotting of blood. The liver plays a key role in the digestive process. Among its other activities it produces and distributes bile, which aids in the absorption of fats into the body and serves as a medium for excreting harmful substances which the liver removes from the blood. When damaged, the liver can regenerate its own tissue immediately.

The kidneys filter the water for our system, retain the good, and pass the waste on to the bladder. The lungs dispose of carbon dioxide. The skin through perspiration not only eliminates waste products but also eliminates excess heat from the body. Our body has the finest waste-disposal system ever created. This cooperative arrangement could not possibly be the result of an infinitude of accidental chance. It too had to have a Creator.

Respiratory System: Breathing

Breathing in oxygen and breathing out carbon dioxide is an essential life process. A number of organs are involved in this process: nostrils, nasal passages, pharynx, trachea, bronchi, bronchial tubes, and lungs. When air is breathed, in the ribs, the rib muscles, diaphragm, and abdominal muscles further cooperate by expanding with the chest. As the air enters the nostrils, tiny hairs filter it. As it passes through the length of the nasal passages, it is thus warmed before entering the trachea. Through the pharynx it goes to the trachea which is lined with cilia which move dust or dirt taken in the air up and out. Then come the bronchi and bronchial tubes, which end in tiny air cells.

These air cells compose most of the lung tissue. They enable the lungs to have a large surface area by which to better supply the body cells with oxygen. The lungs in entirety are composed of these cells, air tubes, blood vessels, and capillaries. Deoxygenated blood is carried to the lungs and returned to the heart purified and filled with oxygen, from thence to be sent all over the body. This respiratory system of ours is a greater invention than any air-conditioning system in existence and performs a far more complex task!

Reproductive System : Making of a Baby

One microscopic cell—the result of a union between a female ovum and a male sperm—is the inauspicious start of a complete human being! All that a human being may be, all his heredity, all his potentiality, all his body and framework, lie within that tiny cell! That one fertilized cell begins to divide and becomes two cells. It continues its division and growth until ultimately it becomes 30 trillion cells! It becomes the complicated physical and mental structure called man.

The 30 trillion cells that come from that one cell become specialists of every kind. Some of them are skin cells, some heart cells, some kidney cells, some brain cells. This is a creation never yet equaled by man, and there is just no comparison!

In the original egg cell, as well as in every living cell, scientists have discovered what they call DNA. They are now convinced that these DNA tapes carry all the coded directions for the construction of each particular person and each particular portion of the body. Those in the fertilized egg cell carry all the hereditary factors from each parent. Although the cell itself is invisible to the naked eye, some DNA experts estimate that if these tapes were rolled out they would extend five feet!

Dr. George W. Beadle, retired chancellor of the University of Chicago and a DNA authority, says that if the coded DNA instructions of a single human cell were put into English, they would fill a 1,000-volume encyclopedia!

It is amazing how many highly educated men attribute the creation of man to pure chance in the light of all the astounding evidence at hand today! Such otherwise intelligent men would never think of attributing the invention of the tape recorder or the composition of an encyclopedia to chance of nature. Yet this DNA tape that has been discovered to be the basis of the making of each man (and of every living thing) is by far more ingenious than any magnetic recording tape man has invented.

GLANDULAR SYSTEM

The glandular system is the vital system in every person that acts like the balance wheel of a watch. The glands control many essential functions of the body. If one of the important glands does not perform its work properly, it vitally affects a person's growth or health in some way. The ductless or endocrine glands pour their essential secretions (hormones) directly into the bloodstream, which carries them to all parts of the body. They thus influence the activity of every organ.

The maintenance of a normal level of thyroid hormone is essential for normal functions of the body. In early infancy it gives the body the immunity mechanism with which the body defends itself against infection from bacteria and invasion by foreign substances. The parathyroid glands control the use of calcium in the body, aid bone growth, muscle tone, and normal nervous activity.

The thymus gland, once thought to be a useless vestigial organ, has been recently discovered (along with other so-called vestigial organs like the tonsils and appendix) to play a major part in the body's defense system. Indeed, it has turned out to be the master gland that regulates the intricate immunity system which protects us against infectious diseases.*

God may have revealed in 1 Corinthians 12:22 what it has taken doctors and scientists all these thousands of years to discover: "Nay, much more those members

---

*See "The 'Useless' Gland That Guards Our Health," *Reader's Digest*, Nov. 1966, pp.229 ff.

of the body, which seem to be more feeble, are necessary." The pituitary hormone stimulates the thyroid and activates the adrenals. It is another growth hormone, affecting sexual development and regulating many important functions of the body.

The adrenal glands vastly increase one's strength and ability during times of stress. They send out a rush of excretions that supercharge a person's body and brain when the need is greatest. Many other glands all over the body quietly and efficiently do their work, each one a miracle of design from the Creator's hand.

Nervous System

Flash! Brain to feet—brain to feet—move! The feet pick themselves up immediately and start running. Every other part of the body is instantly coordinated with the order from the brain. This is far greater than any telephone system, for millions of cells are coordinated in a second to do the brain's bidding. This is our incomparable nervous system! Besides the conscious signals that come from the brain to the body through the nervous system, this extraordinary system of ours also directs all the other vital activities of the body: digestion, respiration, circulation, excretion.

Millions of messages pour through our nervous system to billions of cells day and night. From the brain to the spinal cord and so on out to every part of the body these signals go. What a wondrous communication system!

Sense Organs

From all over our bodies the nervous system conveys to the brain feelings of touch, pain, heat, cold, or pressure. Through these senses of feeling we are warned of impending danger, urged to put on heavy clothing or see a doctor, or moved to think of wedding bells.

The sense of taste enhances our lives with sweet, salty, sour, or bitter flavors. Just think of the sense of enjoyment in food that we would lose without our precious sense of taste! Was not it good of the Lord to give us those 3,000 sensitive little taste buds on our tongues? The sense of smell also helps us to enjoy our food. Without it many foods would lose their flavor for us. It helps us to become aware of danger, as well as to enjoy the fragrances of God's lovely flowers. Each of these blessed senses is a miracle.

God gave us two ears with which to hear on each side of our body. How difficult it would be for us to communicate with each other without them! Extremely sensitive, they can hear a faint whisper. Yet they are so sturdily constructed that they can stand great booms of sound. They are equipped with such a keen sense of selectivity that they can detect the sound of a flute in an orchestra, or one voice in a crowd.

Sound waves start vibrations in the eardrums which are carried by certain small bones to the fluid in the inner ear. The vibrations continue to the auditory nerves, going through a complex process, in order to increase less forceful vibrations to greater amplitude. The vibrations are translated into electrical impulses which, in turn, are translated into meanings by the brain.

Did hearing devices come into existence by themselves? Or did radar evolve by itself from radio? Truly the human ear is even a more complicated instrument than any of these.

What a great blessing our eyesight is, yet how we take it for granted! The nearest star (besides the sun) is 24 trillion miles away, yet our eyes can see it. The eye can send a thousand million impulses to the brain in a second, and the brain chooses significant details of that which is seen.

Our eyeballs are little cameras which focus themselves automatically. They come complete with automatic shutters to protect them and liquids to keep them in good condition. An image focused by the lens falls on the retina back of the eyeball, a retina with about 130 million cells. It receives and records a continually changing, moving picture. Where did the amazing inventions of the camera, moving pictures, and television come from? Well, they certainly were invented by brilliant men, but these men took their great ideas from a previous creation, the human eye.

The lens glass of the human eye is clear and perfectly curved. It changes its curvature automatically to focus on near objects as well as on distant ones. Originally God made the eyes of man perfect, but through the centuries disease and misuse have brought into the human race such defects as nearsightedness and farsightedness. Intelligent men have invented eyeglasses to correct these defects. No one would ever say that eyeglasses came into existence by themselves. Therefore, we cannot consistently say that the eyes themselves did so. They, too, had a master Optician!

THE BRAIN

"Who hath put wisdom in the inward parts? Or who hath given understanding to the heart?" (Job 38:36). Dr. Henry Fairfield Osborn, noted modern anthropologist, said, "To my mind the human brain is the most marvelous and mysterious object in the whole universe."

What are the mechanisms involved in consciousness, thought, behavior, perception, memory? They are still relatively unknown. Although the brain only weighs 3.3 pounds, its work and capacity are far more comprehensive than a telephone exchange requiring 500 tons of equipment.

The mind of man directs the activity of his entire body through over one billion nerve cells. It remembers the past, plans for the future, makes decisions, and carries them out. Man can imagine, dream, think, and reason. He wants to know "why" from childhood. He is inventive, quizzical, logical, and creative. He can absorb fantastic amounts of knowledge, for one human brain is capable of holding more information than the entire nine million volumes in the Library of Congress!

We think that the electronic brain is a marvelous invention of the present day, and it truly is. Yet, the human brain not only comes to a solution with the information at hand, but it also plots a subsequent course of action and activates the body to follow it through. Man can learn to do almost anything. Try to think of all the things man can do that no other creature on earth can do! Man has with his 3.3 pound brain thought up unbelievable inventions that have blessed and helped the world of mankind. He has created works of art, literature, and music that have inspired men down through the centuries.

The cerebrum is the seat of our consciousness, reason, memory, and imagination. It sifts and decodes messages to the brain, then sends decisions and orders to appropriate stations in the body. It handles equally well thousands of pieces of varied information. Each of 10 billion neurons in the brain receive connections from about 100 other neurons. These in turn receive them from another 100. This amazing interconnection enables our brains to work in complete coordination. Truly the brain is by far the most complicated machine in existence!

Fred Kohler, well-known evolutionist, stated: "Primates [apes and their relatives] cannot be taught language to an appreciable extent. . . . [They] lack the necessary organs and nervous equipment. . . . Even if animals are brought up among human beings, they develop no language whatsoever."

Adam, the first man created by God, was given the task of naming all the other creatures on earth. He was the first gardener, and his sons were the first farmers and shepherds. His great-grandchildren (several times removed) invented the first musical instruments and were the first to work with iron and brass (Gen 4:21-22).

Ancient Greeks, Egyptians, and Babylonians were

just as intelligent as people are today. The Egyptians built the famous pyramids with mathematical precision that astounds the engineers of our day. They knew the secret of embalming the dead so that their mummies are still in existence and have not crumbled to dust! The Greeks had a mighty civilization, and their works of art and philosophy have had a profound influence on the world of men for several thousand years. The Babylonians had everything from plumbing to libraries, and they built one of the seven wonders of the world: the famous Hanging Gardens of Babylon.

Yet, today, thousands of years after these great civilizations have passed away, there are still people who live as primitively as the so-called cavemen in South America, Africa, India, and China. When these primitive people are educated, some become the wisest and ablest leaders in our present-day world. The obvious conclusion is that man was endowed from the beginning by his Creator with the same basic intelligence that he has today.

The Greatest Man Who Ever Lived

Let this mind be in you, which was also in Christ Jesus: who, being in the form of God, thought it not robbery to be equal with God: but made himself of no reputation, and took upon him the form of a servant, and was made in the likeness of men: and being found in fashion as a man, he humbled himself, and became obedient unto death, even the death of the cross. Wherefore God also hath highly exalted him, and given him a name which is above every name: that at the name of Jesus every knee should bow . . . and that every tongue should confess that Jesus Christ is Lord, to the glory of God the Father (Phil 2:5-11).

There can be no other spiritual application for the subject of man than the highest one ever given by God Himself. For God the Son humbled Himself and came to earth as a lowly man to reconcile His beloved creatures to Himself. We cannot even begin to imagine the great love of God that He would be willing to give up His glory in heaven to live a hard life here on earth and die an ignominious death!

Jesus Christ was the only perfect man who ever lived. The reason the virgin birth is so vital to true Christianity is that all men are conceived in sin, and the sin principle comes down through the father from Adam. But Jesus was "that holy thing" of God (Lk 1:35), conceived by the Holy Spirit in Mary the virgin (Lk 1:34-35), the only begotten Son of God (Jn 3:16). In order for Jesus Christ to redeem mankind with sinless blood, He had to be born without sin in His blood (which comes from the father) as well as live without sinning. Only then would He be able to present the perfect sacrifice for our sins.

The Son of God completely identified Himself with every member of the human race. He was born in the most humble place that any man was ever born in: a cow manger. He was raised in the lowly home of a carpenter and probably developed fine muscles carrying loads of wood for Joseph. He was born in a time and place that knew nothing of the conveniences we enjoy today. His chief diet consisted of fish and bread.

He allowed Himself to be tempted by the god of this world, Satan. By permitting this, He further identified Himself with mankind in that we too are tempted. Although He had disappeared several times before when the people tried to kill Him, when the proper time came Jesus Christ permitted men to take Him to His death. Although He had healed the blind, cleansed the lepers, and raised the dead, He permitted men to spit on Him, scourge Him, and nail Him to a cruel cross.

They slammed the cross down between the crosses of two thieves. And Jesus hung there, willingly paying the awful penalty for our sins. In one terrible moment Jesus cried out, "My God, my God, why hast thou forsaken me?" As the crushing weight and penalty of our sins were laid on Jesus Christ, God the Father had to turn His back for the only time in eternity on God the Son! Thunder crashed, lightning split the pitch blackness of that day, the earth shook, and graves opened. The veil in the Jewish Temple that hid the sanctuary of God from the people was rent from top to bottom.

And standing near the cross, looking up with awe, the Roman centurion exclaimed, "Truly this man was the Son of God!"

12

THE NEW CREATION

> Therefore if any man be in Christ, he is a new creature: old things are passed away; behold, all things are become new (2 Co 5:17).

THE OLD CHINESE MAN was at the end of his rope and knew it. Twenty-three stays at sanitariums had failed to cure him of the opium habit. Steeped to the eyeballs in dope and liquor, he had stumbled into a warm New York City mission to get out of the cold. Exhausted and bleary eyed, he sank gratefully into a pew near the back of the hall.

Music and singing started to fill the air. Someone poked him and said, "Hey, stand up!" Groggily he stood to his feet. Words of the song came through his fogged consciousness. "Would you be free from the burden of sin? There's power in the blood, power in the blood. . . . Would you o'er evil the victory win? There's wonderful power in the blood. . . ."

What does it mean? he wondered. *Is there help for me after all?*

During the service he tried to pay attention to all that was being said, but it was hard to concentrate in his sodden state. Several men stood and told how they had been freed from their slavery to liquor. A tiny flame of hope began to burn in the Chinese man's breast.

A man stood up to speak from behind the pulpit, a man with a black book in his hand. He talked about someone named Jesus Christ who had come to earth to die for men's sins so that they might have eternal life. He had shed His blood to cleanse men's souls so that they would be right with God. If anyone accepted this Son of God as his Saviour, he would be born into God's family and become a new person. He could have victory over the things of the world that enslaved him!

The Chinese man leaned forward, striving eagerly to catch every important word. Another hymn was announced and everyone stood up. The preacher said, "If God has spoken to your heart tonight and you would like Jesus Christ to save you, won't you come forward while this hymn is being sung?"

The Chinese man lowered his head briefly. Should he go forward? Was there hope for him, even him? His heart had been stirred greatly as he had heard about this magnificent Jesus Christ. He made his decision. Pushing his way out of the pew, he stumbled forward and fell on his face before the altar.

It was several days before the mission superintendent was able to bring this poor wreck of a human being out of the terrible state induced by opium and liquor. Finally, when the man came to, he looked for a moment at the superintendent without comprehension of where he was. The superintendent put his hand gently on his shoulder and asked, "Did you mean it the other night when you came forward to accept Christ?"

Remembrance flooded back and the Chinese man grasped the superintendent's hand. "Oh, yes!" he exclaimed. "But I have one question."

"And what is that?" asked the superintendent.

"Did Jesus Christ die for the Chinese too?" he asked eagerly.

"Yes," affirmed the superintendent, "Jesus Christ died for all men of all colors and races."

"Then I want Him for my Saviour," the man said simply.

As he and the superintendent prayed together, tears began to stream down the Chinese man's face. As he lifted it, it was radiant with joy. From that day on he never had to have any opium or liquor. He had not only been saved from eternal death but also miraculously saved from the terrible cravings of his own body! Truly he was a "new creature in Christ."

But the deprivation his body had gone through for years because of his habits had finally taken its toll. Doctors found that he had tuberculosis, so he was sent to the state sanitarium for cure. There he became an inspiration to all who came into contact with him, for he was a faithful missionary for Jesus Christ. Many there in his mission field, the sanitarium, have come to know Jesus Christ and to obtain eternal life through this former slave to opium and alcohol. The life at the end of the rope had become a channel of blessing and hope!

This same transformation has taken place to a greater or lesser degree in the life of every person who has truly accepted Christ as his Saviour. Drunkards have become mission superintendents, juvenile delinquents have become missionaries, criminals have become evangelists, people from all walks of life and backgrounds have become dedicated Christians because of the transforming power of Jesus Christ.

This is the new birth; this is God's new creation! Probably most of us, before we were born into God's family, knew someone who testified to the tremendous transformation wrought in his life. But since I have been saved I have met hundreds of people with such thrilling stories. The new birth is not turning over a new leaf; it is not joining a church or being baptized. It is a creative work of God done in the heart of a person when he accepts Christ as Saviour.

Many people think that in order to be saved they have to give up dancing, smoking, theater going, drinking, or various other things. They probably get this idea from the fact that they know people who have been saved who have relinquished some or all of these things. Such an idea is not true. But they do have to come to the Lord with a wholehearted desire to turn their lives over to Him.

When a person comes to Christ, his whole viewpoint is changed. Because he has a new spirit within him, he now wants to live his life for Jesus Christ rather than for himself. He takes a long look at his old life and suddenly finds many things in it which are distasteful and inconsistent with what he wants his Christian testimony to be. Many things that once appealed to him now lose their appeal; and he suddenly acquires a great thirst for things that once he had no time for, such as prayer and Bible study. New Christian friends take the place of old carousing friends. He is now the temple of God, for God is dwelling in him.

Some may ask, "Well, if this new creation is true, why aren't the Christians I know perfect?"

There are two answers. First, have they truly been born again into God's family, or are they merely professing Christians? Second, even if they are true Christians, some of the old nature still remains in them because they are still in the fleshly body. Instant deliverance from slavery to dope or drink occurs in many cases, such as for the Chinese man. But in many other cases it takes some period of time for the Holy Spirit to work in a new Christian's life before he is able to relinquish some cherished or fixed habits. In no case is every vestige of sin completely wiped out, but rather in every case the Holy Spirit works through a lifetime in order to conform Christians to the image of Christ (Ro 8:29; Phil 1:6). Paul exhorted the Ephesian Christians:

> That ye put off concerning the former conversation [way of life] the old man, which is corrupt according to the deceitful lusts; and be renewed in the spirit of your mind; and that ye put on the new man, which after God is created in righteousness and true holiness (Eph 4:22-24).

This old man and new man, then, are like two suits of clothing hanging in the heart's closet of a Christian.

Every part of the old suit is to be put off, and the new suit is to be put on. As we yield ourselves to the Lord, His Spirit points out some of the old shreds that are still hanging on in our lives. As we read and hear God's Word, the Spirit uses it to convict us of "the old man" shreds.

Man is the first thing in the world to be made into a new creation. Someday, the Bible promises, all things will be made new. The Book of Revelation says:

> And I saw a new heaven and a new earth: for the first heaven and the first earth were passed away; and there was no more sea. And I John saw the holy city, new Jerusalem, coming down from God out of heaven, prepared as a bride adorned for her husband. And I heard a great voice out of heaven saying, Behold, the tabernacle of God is with men, and he will dwell with them, and they shall be his people, and God himself shall be with them, and be their God. And God shall wipe away all tears from their eyes; and there shall be no more death, neither sorrow, nor crying, neither shall there be any more pain: for the former things are passed away (Rev 21:1-4).

In that day we shall have our new resurrection bodies like unto that of our Lord Jesus Christ. Then our bodies shall be redeemed from the bondage of corruption, just as our spirits are now. As the apostle Paul wrote:

> And as we have borne the image of the earthy, we shall also bear the image of the heavenly.... Behold, I shew you a mystery; we shall not all sleep, but we shall all be changed. In a moment, in the twinkling of an eye, at the last trump: for the trumpet shall sound,

and the dead shall be raised incorruptible, and we shall be changed. For this corruptible must put on incorruption, and this mortal must put on immortality. . . . Death is swallowed up in victory. O death, where is thy sting? O grave, where is thy victory? . . . But thanks be to God, which giveth us the victory through our Lord Jesus Christ (1 Co 15:49-57).

BIBLIOGRAPHY

Adler, Irving. *Dust*. New York: John Day, 1958.

Anderson, A. W. *Plants of the Bible*. New York: Philosophical Lib., 1957.

Berry, George Ricker. *The Inter-Linear Hebrew-English Old Testament—Genesis-Exodus*. Grand Rapids: Zondervan, 1951.

Bush, George. *Bush's Notes, Genesis*. Vol. 1. New York: Newman & Ivison, 1852.

Carson, Rachel L. *The Sea Around Us*. New York: Oxford, 1961.

Davis, John D. and Gehman, Henry Snyder. *Westminster Dictionary of the Bible*. Philadelphia: Westminster, 1944.

Day, Lewis. *Nature and Ornament*. New York: Scribner's, 1929.

DeHann, M. R. *The Chemistry of the Blood*. 8th ed. Grand Rapids: Zondervan, 1943.

DeVoe, Allen. *This Fascinating Animal World*. New York: McGraw-Hill, 1951.

Heinroth, Oskar and Heinroth, Katharina. *The Birds*. 2d ed. Ann Arbor, Mich.: U. Mich., 1955.

Henry, Matthew. *Matthew Henry's Commentary on the New Testament*. New York: Revell, 1961.

Hoyle, Fred. *Frontiers of Astronomy*. New York: Harper & Bros., 1955.

Lane, Ferdinand C. *The Story of Trees*. Garden City, N. Y.: Doubleday, 1952.

Meldau, John Fred. *Why We Believe in Creation*. Denver: Christian Victory, 1959.

Moon, Truman J.; Mann, Paul B.; and Otto, James H. *Modern Biology*. New York: Henry Holt, 1951.

Morris, Henry. *Studies in the Bible and Science*. Philadelphia: Presby. & Ref., 1966.

Morris, Percy A. *They Hop and Crawl*. Lancaster, Pa.: Jaques Cattell, 1944.

The New Wonder Book: Cyclopedia of World Knowledge. Philadelphia: International, 1954.

Rehwinkel, Alfred M. *The Flood*. St. Louis: Concordia, 1957.

Rimmer, Harry. *The Harmony of Science and Scripture*. 5th ed. Grand Rapids: Eerdmans, 1936.

—————————. *The Theory of Evolution and the Facts of Science*. 10th ed. Grand Rapids: Eerdmans, 1954.

Robinson, John. *The Universe We Live In*. New York: Thomas Y. Crowell, 1951.

Sanden, O. E. *Does Science Support the Scriptures?* Grand Rapids: Zondervan, 1951.

Simpson, F. Y. *Spiritual Interpretation of Nature*. 3d ed. London: Hodder & Stoughton, 1923.

Strong, James. *Strong's Exhaustive Concordance of the Bible*. New York: Abingdon, 1890.

Tournier, Paul. *The Meaning of Persons*. New York: Harper & Bros., 1957.

Verrill, A. Hyatt. *Wonder Plants and Plant Wonders*. New York: Appleton-Century, 1939.

Wentworth, H. A. *Scientific Analysis of the Bible*. Newark, N. J., 1951.

Whitcomb, John, Jr., and Morris, Henry. *The Genesis Flood*. Philadelphia: Presby. & Ref., 1961.